Inside the Common Core Classroom

Inside the Common Core Classroom

Practical ELA Strategies for Grades 6–8

Maureen McLaughlin

East Stroudsburg University

PEARSON

Boston • Columbus • Indianapolis • New York • San Francisco • Upper Saddle River
Amsterdam • Cape Town • Dubai • London • Madrid • Milan • Munich • Paris • Montréal • Toronto
Delhi • Mexico City • São Paulo • Sydney • Hong Kong • Seoul • Singapore • Taipei • Tokyo

Vice President and Editorial Director: Jeffery Johnston
Acquisitions Editor: Kathryn Boice
Editorial Assistant: Carolyn Schweitzer
Executive Field Marketing Manager: Krista Clark
Senior Product Marketing Manger: Christopher Barry
Program Manager: Karen Mason
Project Manager: Barbara Strickland
Editorial Production Service: Electronic Publishing Services Inc., NYC
Manufacturing Buyer: Linda Sager
Electronic Composition: Jouve
Project Coordination & Interior Design: Electronic Publishing Services Inc., NYC
Photo Researcher: Jorgensen Fernandez
Cover Designer: Central Covers

Library of Congress Cataloging-in-Publication Data

McLaughlin, Maureen.
  Inside the common core classroom : practical ELA strategies for grades 6-8 / Maureen McLaughlin.
      p. cm.
  Includes bibliographical references and index.
  ISBN 978-0-13-336353-1
1. Language arts (Middle school)—Standards—United States—States.   I. Title.
  LB1631.M39533 2015
  428.0071'2—dc23

                                                                      2013046084

10 9 8 7 6 5 4 3 2 1

ISBN 10:   0-13-336353-8
ISBN 13: 978-0-13-336353-1

Dedication

- *For Tracy Reidinger, Kimberly McFadden, Alexandria Gibb Lucas, and all teachers of the Common Core.*

Contents

chapter 7 *Curriculum Implications*   **143**

Preface

WELCOME TO THE AGE OF THE COMMON CORE! Thank you for joining us in our quest to teach students to meet the Common Core English Language Arts (ELA) Standards.

This volume, *Inside the Common Core Classroom: Practical ELA Strategies for Grades 6–8,* is part of Pearson's *College and Career Readiness Series.* The books in this series have been written for in-service teachers to support their implementation of the Common Core State Standards for English language arts in K–12 classrooms. The four volumes in the series address the standards in grades K–2, 3–5, 6–8, and 9–12, respectively.

The purpose of the series is to help teachers create connections between the Common Core and their school curriculums. Each book provides in-depth information about the standards at a particular grade-level band and offers examples of a variety of teaching ideas to support students' meeting the expectations of the ELA Standards.

About This Book

This book is structured to provide essential information about the Common Core, insights into the Standards, practical classroom strategies, and vignettes from inside Common Core classrooms. An interdisciplinary unit completes the work.

The book begins with an overview authored by series editor, Donna Ogle. Donna discusses the origin of the Common Core initiative and chronicles its development and implementation.

Chapter 1 narrows its focus to the English Language Arts Standards, grades 6–8, including the College and Career Readiness Anchor Standards and the Common Core State Standards. Also discussed are the language of the Common Core, formative and summative assessment, and what is and what is not included in the Common Core Standards.

Chapter 2 looks at how the Common Core relates to reading comprehension, what is known about reading comprehension, and which strategy applications can be used to effectively teach it. A variety of teaching ideas in subsequent chapters also support students' reading comprehension.

Chapter 3 explores the CCSS and vocabulary. Details from the standards, current knowledge about teaching vocabulary, and practical teaching ideas are all included.

Chapter 4 addresses text complexity and features the Common Core Model.

Chapter 5 is dedicated to the Common Core Speaking and Listening Standards. In this chapter, multiple ways to integrate speaking and listening in teaching and learning are explored and projects, such as Press Conference and Debate, are delineated.

The focus of Chapter 6 is writing. The Writing Standards and practical teaching ideas are integrated.

Chapter 7 examines how the Common Core State Standards (CCSS) relate to school curriculums. Emphasis is placed on integrating the CCSS, rather than using them to replace existing curriculums.

The book concludes with an appendix, featuring an Interdisciplinary Unit on Climate Change that focuses on the Common Core and the Next Generation Science Standards (2013). English, science, social studies, and the arts are the integrated disciplines. The Common Core State Standards are embedded in the unit, which includes discipline-specific teaching suggestions, sample lesson plans, completed strategies, an assessment and evaluation plan, a culminating activity, and a rich collection of resources.

Teaching and learning in the age of the Common Core is a challenge for all engaged. It is both hopeful and rewarding to note that we are all working together to ensure that our students are college and career ready.

Acknowledgments

As always, there are many people to thank for making this book possible. I express appreciation to all who contributed to the manuscript's development as well as all who enhanced the quality of my life during the research and writing process. I thank them for their insight, their understanding, and their support.

I am particularly grateful to the following people:

Tracy Reidinger, Kimberly McFadden, and Alexandria Gibb

Angela Britton, Andy Crawford, Daniel Marx, and Ezra Shapiro

Kathryn Boice, Acquisitions Editor at Pearson Education

Barbara Strickland, Project Manager at Pearson Education

Carrie Fox, Lead Content Project Manager at Electronic Publishing Services Inc., NYC

Finally, I would like to thank the reviewers for this first edition: Theresa A. Barone, Derby Middle School (MI); Jane H. Crowley, Maine School Administrative District #51; Susan Grinsteinner, River Oaks Middle School (SC); Bonnie Dezern Olson, East Hardin Middle School (KY); and Bari Stalder, Chapman Middle School (KS).

Inside the Common Core Classroom

Introduction

Donna Ogle

THE COMMON CORE STATE STANDARDS (CCSS) are a challenging set of expectations that students must meet to be college and career ready. According to the Common Core, all educators are responsible for teaching literacy. To support this thinking, the CCSS English Language Arts (ELA) Standards include literacy in science, social studies, and technical subjects. These standards support the importance of integrating reading, writing, and speaking and listening in the disciplines. The ELA Common Core State Standards invite teachers to work together within and across grade levels and content areas to ensure that students will meet the expectations delineated in the standards.

Across the United States, the national, state, and local organizations that have taken this challenge seriously are in the process of analyzing current curricula and adjusting the focus of instruction and expected student outcomes according to these new needs and demands. The two national assessment consortia—the Partnership for Assessment of Readiness for College and Career (PARCC, n.d.) and SMARTER Balance (n.d.)—are in the process of designing new assessment systems, which will be administered for the first time during the 2014–2015 school year. These consortia have suggested how school curricula should be organized to encompass the broad-reaching outcomes elaborated in the CCSS. Taking the CCSS seriously means making some significant adjustments in how our schools have focused on literacy and the kinds of literacy-related opportunities they have provided. Our students deserve this support. They want to be successful both within and beyond schooling, and we want them to have this success.

Defining the Need for the Change

THE CCSS DESCRIBE IN GRADE-BY-GRADE DETAIL THE WIDE range of competencies that literacy entails and that teachers need to develop in their students. The starting point for this effort is central to the standards' importance: What is required of students to be college and career ready?

Several research reports over the last decade have alerted interested educators to the decline in difficulty of many school texts and to the challenge faced by students with low reading proficiency when they take college-level tests. In fact, Appendix A of the CCSS cites a 2006 ACT report, *Reading Between the Lines,* to illustrate this two-part problem (NGA & CCSSO, 2010b, Appendix A, p. 2). Recognizing this problem led the developers of the CCSS to collect texts being used by students in freshmen-level college/university courses and by individuals entering the workforce after high school. These texts were compared with high school texts and the types and difficulty levels of assigned student work.

In this analysis, the CCSS developers identified a significant gap between the work required of upper-level high school students and the expectations for success in college and career. (See Appendix A of the CCSS for elaboration on this issue [NGA & CCSSO, 2010b].) The CCSS were then developed with this end point in mind: to determine the level of language arts development needed at each grade level for students to be prepared for these greater literacy demands and thus ready for college and career.

After the CCSS had been written, they were reviewed by college faculty who teach freshman- and sophomore-level courses, who gave the standards high marks. Interestingly, in addition to the need for students to read informational texts critically and to write effective analytical essays (not personal reflection pieces), these faculty rated the oral communication skills identified in the CCSS as particularly important.

The fact that perspectives from higher education and the workforce were included in developing the CCSS is important. The standards make this connection very clear: Students need to be college and career ready.

The CCSS are significant in another way, also. Since the first round of standards was developed in the late 1990s, individual states have crafted their own standards and measured achievement with their own state-specific assessments. The only comparison of achievement across states has been made by the National Assessment of Educational Progress (NAEP), and these evaluations have regularly revealed huge state-by-state differences in literacy achievement. Now, with the CCSS, we have, for the first time, a set of standards that has been adopted by most states across the country.

This high level of adoption will help all educators evaluate their success and feel confident that their students are receiving a high-quality education that will serve them beyond public school. Both the standards and the assessments being developed can help all educators engage in a shared conversation and commitment to excellence. Rather than relying on the current patchwork of state standards, the CCSS bring together a common set of standards and permit the development of more common assessments.

Expectations for Literacy Achievement

AS THE UNITED STATES MOVES FORWARD WITH THE new standards, all educators need to be involved and take seriously new expectations for the future. The CCSS raise the bar for student literacy achievement in several ways:

- To be college and career ready, students must understand challenging texts and attend to authors' ideas and ways of presenting information. In the CCSS Reading standards, three clusters identify these foci: Key Ideas and Details, Craft and Structure, and Integration of Knowledge and Ideas. For both literature and informational texts, readers are expected to engage in careful reading of the ideas presented, to recall main ideas and details, to recognize the organization of information and author's craft, and to synthesize and critically respond to what they have read.

- This expectation for greater understanding is heightened by the expectation that students will read texts at a more accelerated level of difficulty than currently designated for grade levels by readability formulas and reading anthologies. For twelfth-grade texts, the expected level will be about 200 Lexile points higher than the current level.

- The CCSS also devote greater attention to reading informational text, so it receives the same instructional attention as literature. Most elementary programs and secondary language arts courses have been developed primarily around fictional/narrative literature. The CCSS create a broader framework for literacy development that includes the content areas, especially social studies, science, and technical subjects. With two sets of standards for reading—one for literature and one for informational text—this shift in foci to informational texts and to the importance of using reading to build knowledge is clear. At the secondary level, the CCSS differentiate expectations for literacy development in social studies, science, and technical subjects. The curriculum design from PARCC (n.d.), which establishes four basic modules, includes a balance of informational and literary texts across the modules.

- The CCSS emphasize not only the understanding of individual texts but also the importance of reading across texts to look for different authors' purposes and the evidence authors provide to support their ideas. Students who read only one text on a topic or theme have little opportunity to learn about how authors can vary in terms of purpose and presentation of ideas. The CCSS clearly advocate that students should read several texts on the same topic or theme. In addition, completing quarterly research projects provides individuals with opportunities to search for information across multiple texts and media sources and to use that information in their projects and performances.

- The shift in how information is communicated in the twenty-first century is also recognized in the CCSS. We live in a visual society: All sorts of images try to inform us and persuade us. The ability to use visual and graphic information thoughtfully is expected of students. In fact, visual images can be powerful motivators to engage students in thoughtful analyses of how ideas are communicated to us and influence us. Across the content areas, readers are also expected to use electronic sources in building their knowledge in presenting information and completing research projects.

- There is also a shift in focus in the writing standards from writing personal narratives to writing expository and argumentative texts. Students need to be able to use evidence to support their arguments, as well as to recognize possible alternative points of view. In addition, writing is now being used as a way of measuring students' reading comprehension. Students need to think about the meanings of the texts they read, how authors present and support ideas, and what counter-arguments and evidence are provided.

- Although speaking and listening have always been part of the language arts, the CCSS recognize the importance of these communication tools. This priority is evident in the Speaking and Listening Standards and also embedded in the expectations that students discuss what they read at every grade level and learn to report to classmates what they learn from individual research projects. The preliminary assessment design from PARCC (n.d.) includes a school-based assessment of oral skills midway through the year. Even though these skills are difficult to measure using large-scale assessments, they are important. The value of speaking and listening skills has been well established by the university and workplace communities.

- The CCSS also include expectations for vocabulary. Specifically, students should learn and use standard forms of English and appropriate general academic and domain-specific vocabulary in both writing and oral language. Vocabulary and word-learning strategies need to be developed concurrently with the knowledge and content literacy standards, especially as related to the domain-specific terms students need to know to understand the content of science, social studies, and technical subjects.

Implementing the CCSS

IMPLEMENTING THE CCSS REPRESENTS A SIGNIFICANT CHALLENGE TO teachers and schools. To address the difficulty of this task, many states have put together teams to guide their thinking about what is already being done and what needs to be adjusted in the current curriculum to meet expectations for literacy in the twenty-first century. Other educational organizations have also made significant efforts to help in the development of curriculum and instructional frameworks—for example, the Lucas Foundation, Annenberg Foundation, Alliance for Effective Education, AchieveNY, Gates Foundation, International Reading Association, and National Council of Teachers of English.

Publishers have responded, as well, by reorienting materials to reflect the broader expectation for responding to texts and by including more academic writing and attention to content. An interesting publisher's initiative has brought together teacher teams from school districts and used their materials to reorganize the content and rewrite the questions in the published programs to align more closely with the CCSS.

The major goal of all of these efforts is to better prepare students for college and careers. Doing so requires addressing the range of texts students read, the depth of thinking they do, and the styles of writing they perform. Given these new and challenging expectations, professionals across the educational system need to collaborate in helping students from preschool through grade 12 develop the competencies, commitment, and confidence needed for life beyond high school.

Rethinking the Complexity of the Texts Students Read

The issue of text complexity is central to the CCSS and one that deserves study by teacher and school teams. Students need to engage in more challenging texts at each grade level, at least beyond the primary grades, and they need to read more informational texts, which are rich in content.

The authors of the CCSS have tried to move away from a single, numerically derived formula for determining the appropriate reading levels of texts of all kinds. According to the CCSS, three criteria should be considered when determining the level of any text:

1. **Qualitative evaluation of the text:** levels of meaning, structure, language conventionality and clarity, and knowledge demands

2. **Quantitative evaluation of the text:** readability measures and other scores of text complexity

3. **Matching the reader to the text and the task:** reader variables (e.g., motivation, knowledge, and experiences) and task variables (e.g., the purpose and complexity of the task assigned and the questions posed) (NGA & CCSSO, 2010b, p. 4).

Appendix B of the CCSS (NGA & CCSSO, 2010c) provides lists of illustrative books that have been "leveled." The purpose of these lists is not to imply that these books should be used in the schools but rather to identify books that are familiar to the educational community. However, teachers who want simply to select books from these lists need to remember the third criterion: matching the reader to the text and the task.

Given the variety of interests, experiences, and needs of students across the United States, many teachers will want to use contemporary, high-interest materials to motivate students to think and reflect deeply about important issues. Moreover, instead of permitting students to read only books at their designated levels (based on Lexiles or Fountas & Pinnell scores), teachers will ask students in the intermediate grades and higher to read several books or articles on the same topic, beginning with a comfortable-level book/article and then using the knowledge they have developed to read more difficult texts on the same topic.

Using this strategy is certainly one way to help students increase their reading power. The CCSS guidelines also provide models of how teachers can engage groups of students in close readings of anchor texts or targeted short texts. When teachers regularly model an analytical and questioning approach to reading, students will likely follow the same approach. It is also important that students engage with a large quantity of texts, finding their own favorite authors and experiencing the joy of being real readers.

Organizing Instruction into Content-Rich Units

The range and complexity of literacy standards included in the CCSS has prompted many organizations (e.g., PARCC and SMARTER Balance), as well as school districts and state education departments (e.g., Wisconsin Department of Public Instruction), to reorganize their literacy priorities to align with the CCSS by designing units with content-related themes and topics. Using this approach, instruction in literacy is combined with instruction in social studies and science. Many school districts have asked teams of teachers to develop one unit as a starting point with plans to expand this effort over time.

A clear message from the developers of the CCSS is that students need to be engaged in learning content in social studies, science, and technical subjects at a deeper level than is now often the case. In the CCSS guidelines, the final section about the elementary standards is entitled "Staying on Topic Within a Grade and Across Grades: How to Build Knowledge Systematically in English Language Arts K–5" (NGA & CCSSO, 2010a, p. 33). Included in this section is a matrix illustrating how students should encounter the same topic (in this example, the human body) at increasingly deeper levels across all of the grades. This shift in combining attention to content knowledge with literacy development is one of the hallmarks of the CCSS.

While combining these purposes makes good sense, it means that schools must expand efforts at integrating reading and writing with content area instruction. Classroom and school libraries should contain ample amounts of informational books and magazines at a variety of levels of complexity so that all students have access to the materials needed to develop deep knowledge. As the CCSS authors explain in the section "Staying on Topic Within a Grade and Across Grades":

> Building knowledge systematically in English language arts is like giving children various pieces of a puzzle in each grade that, over time, will form one big picture. At a curricular or instructional level, texts—within and across grade levels—need to be selected around topics or themes that systematically develop the knowledge base of students. Within a grade level, there should be an adequate number of titles on a single topic that would allow children to study that topic for a sustained period. The knowledge children have learned about particular topics in early grade levels should then be expanded and developed in subsequent grade levels to ensure an increasingly deeper understanding of these topics. Children in the upper elementary grades will generally be expected to read these texts independently and reflect on them in writing. However, children in the early grades (particularly K–2) should participate in rich, structured conversations with an adult in response to the written texts that are read aloud, orally comparing and contrasting as well as analyzing and synthesizing, in the manner called for by the *Standards*. (NGA & CCSSO, 2010a, p. 33)

At the secondary level, there is an even greater expectation for students to develop the strategies necessary for reading the varied texts and materials that contain the key content of disciplinary study. Reading primary source documents in history and science is a central part of students' literacy engagement. Also, the texts used in math and science require students to analyze a variety of visual displays, including equations, tables, diagrams, and graphs. As noted in the Carnegie Report *Writing to Read* (Graham & Hebert, 2010), for students to comprehend and produce these types of texts, they must be immersed in the language and thinking processes of these disciplines and they must be supported by an expert guide: their teacher.

Given the expectation for students to develop the competence needed to comprehend the wide variety of texts that is required for success in and beyond schooling, it is clear that the responsibility for literacy development cannot reside solely with English language arts teachers. Meeting this expectation requires both the development of foundational knowledge that makes deep learning possible and the skills needed to read a wide variety of text types and formats across the disciplines. The CCSS challenge all content area teachers to accept their part in developing the literacy skills, dispositions, discipline-specific discourse, and academic vocabulary requisite for students to become independent learners. The more often that elementary and secondary reading/literacy coaches team up with their content area colleagues, the more likely that CCSS goals will be met by providing interesting and positive instructional experiences for students.

The thematic-unit framework provides students with the opportunity to read several texts on the same theme or topic and build their background knowledge of a specific topic. Spending more time on a specific topic also helps students to deepen their knowledge of the content and become familiar with the academic and domain-specific vocabulary central to that learning. In addition, by reading across several texts, students can develop their understanding of the ways different authors select materials to include in particular texts and then organize that information, as well as the value of reading deeply to build clear understanding of complex ideas.

Having these commitments to reading makes students' written and oral communications much stronger. Students know what they are explaining and have options to represent their ideas, including visual, graphic, and oral formats. This ability to develop one's own understanding based on research and then to present one's ideas is woven into the four research projects students are expected to do each year In addition, the CCSS directive to engage in a deeper study of topics encourages teachers to vary the kinds of learning experiences they provide for their students—differentiating texts/materials, activities, products, and assessments (Tomlinson's framework).

Engaging in Schoolwide Collaboration for Change

The challenges and cross-content literacy expectations of the CCSS can be achieved within a long-range timeframe and with the understanding that they will develop over the course of students' schooling. Realizing these requisites for achievement can unite teachers. The CCSS underscore the importance of involving teams of educators representing all grade levels, special services (e.g., English language learning, special education, library and media), and content areas in studying the CCSS, analyzing their implications, and designing ways to implement them over time.

Discussing the CCSS across grade levels is a good way to start. Providing visual displays that trace the same standard across different grades will help teachers to understand the structure and rationale that underlie the CCSS. An example follows using Standard 3 of the grades 6–12 Anchor Standards for Reading, which appears in the category Key Ideas and Ideas:

> **Standard 3:** Analyze how and why individuals, events, and ideas develop and interact over the course of a text.

Table I.1 shows the grade-level expectations for Standard 3 for reading literature and informational text across grades 6–12. The table also shows expectations at grades 6–8, 9–10, and 11–12 for the same standard for literacy in history/social studies and in science and technical subjects. Creating and reviewing a chart of this nature allows examination of the expectations across grades.

Clearly, within Standard 3, there is a gradual progression of difficulty from sixth through twelfth grade—both within the same standard and across its application in different contexts. At first, differences in expectations may seem somewhat arbitrary, but looking across grade levels and text types reveals increasingly more complex expectations for students' ability to use the ideas and information that authors develop.

TABLE I.1 ● *CCSS Reading Standard 3, Key Ideas and Details:* Grades 6–12

Reading Standards for Literature

Grade 6 students:	Grade 7 students:	Grade 8 students:
3. Describe how a particular story's or drama's plot unfolds in a series of episodes as well as how the characters respond or change as the plot moves toward a resolution.	3. Analyze how particular elements of a story or drama interact (e.g., how setting shapes the characters or plot).	3. Analyze how particular lines of dialogue or incidents in a story or drama propel the action, reveal aspects of a character, or provoke a decision.

Grades 9–10 students:	Grades 11–12 students:
3. Analyze how complex characters (e.g., those with multiple or conflicting motivations) develop over the course of a text, interact with other characters, and advance the plot or develop the theme.	3. Analyze the impact of the author's choices regarding how to develop and relate elements of a story or drama (e.g., where a story is set, how the action is ordered, how the characters are introduced and developed).

(continued)

TABLE I.1 ● *(continued)*
Reading Standards for Informational Text

Grade 6 students:	Grade 7 students:	Grade 8 students:
3. Analyze in detail how a key individual, event, or idea is introduced, illustrated, and elaborated in a text (e.g., through examples or anecdotes.	3. Analyze the interactions between individuals, events, and ideas in a text (e.g., how ideas influence individuals or events, or how individuals influence ideas or events).	3. Analyze how a text makes connections among and distinctions between individuals, ideas, or events (e.g., through comparisons, analogies, or categories).

Grades 9–10 students:	Grades 11–12 students:
3. Analyze how the author unfolds an analysis or series of ideas or events, including the order in which the points are made, how they are introduced and developed, and the connections that are drawn between them.	3. Analyze a complex set of ideas or sequence of events and explain how specific individuals, ideas, or events interact and develop over the course of the text.

Reading Standards for Literacy in History/Social Studies

Grades 6–8 students:	Grades 9–10 students:	Grades 11–12 students:
3. Identify key steps in a text's description of a process related to history/social studies (e.g., how a bill becomes law, how interest rates are raised or lowered).	3. Analyze in detail a series of events described in a text; determine whether earlier events caused later ones or simply preceded them.	3. Evaluate various explanations for actions or events and determine which explanation best accords with textual evidence, acknowledging where the text leaves matters uncertain.

Reading Standards for Literacy in Science and Technical Subjects

Grades 6–8 students:	Grades 9–10 students:	Grades 11–12 students:
3. Follow precisely a multistep procedure when carrying out experiments, taking measurements, or performing technical tasks.	3. Follow precisely a complex multistep procedure when carrying out experiments, taking measurements, or performing technical tasks, attending to special cases or exceptions defined in the text.	3. Follow precisely a complex multistep procedure when carrying out experiments, taking measurements, or performing technical tasks; analyze the specific results based on explanations in the text.

Sharing an analysis and discussion of instructional expectations can build a common language and focus among teachers. Moreover, it can provide a good starting point for conversations about the evidence that demonstrates what skills and knowledge students already have and what areas need to be developed to ensure ongoing progress in the important area of reading comprehension. Teachers at no one grade level are responsible for the mastery of any standard, but across the grades and content areas, teachers should guide students in applying reading skills to increasingly challenging and varied materials and contexts. By looking across grade levels and disciplines, teachers can work together to identify ways to help students develop their abilities to think broadly about how authors develop and connect ideas in the varied types of texts they read during their secondary school years.

Just as it is important for teams of teachers to look at the standards' expectations for skill development across the grades, it is important for them to read across the areas within the CCSS. In contrast to the orientation in some districts and schools, in which teaching focuses on one standard at a time, the areas within the CCSS are interrelated and build on each other. Not only are standards provided for both literature and informational text, but in addition, many key expectations are scattered across the reading, writing, and language standards and the literacy standards for history/social studies and science and technical subjects. For example, a category called Integration of Knowledge and Ideas is included in the standards for Reading Literature and Reading Informational Text, as well as in the Reading Standards for Literacy in History/Social Studies and the Reading Standards for Literacy in Science and Technical Subjects. Similar connections pertain to skills in reading texts of various types and complexities, conducting research and applying its findings, and writing for a variety of tasks, purposes, and audiences.

The Speaking and Listening Standards address the importance of students creating visual and media displays. In the past, visual and media literacy seem to have been the purview of secondary instruction, but in the CCSS, they are introduced in the early elementary grades. Providing this early start allows greater development of speaking and listening skills. In grades 6–12, the focus of the Speaking and Listening standards is on preparing students to be college and career ready.

Some important instructional areas that teachers are accustomed to seeing as parts of reading development are embedded elsewhere in the CCSS. Vocabulary, for example, does not have a separate set of standards, as do reading literature and writing, yet developing vocabulary skills is very important and is addressed in several sections of the CCSS. Teacher teams might begin by studying the Language Standards section Vocabulary Acquisition and Use, with its focus on learning academic and domain-specific vocabulary, and then locate other places in the standards where vocabulary skills are addressed. Once again, for grades 6–12, the standards focus on preparing students to be college and career ready.

In addition, teacher teams need to consider carefully the expectation to include science, history/social studies, and technical subjects that is part of their responsibility in implementing these new more content-focused standards. Some states, such as

Wisconsin, have developed their own extensions of the CCSS (Wisconsin Department of Public Instruction, n.d.), and these models can provide valuable resources as school teams examine their curriculum options and make decisions about how to move forward. Moreover, the CCSS for grades 6–12 include sets of standards for reading and writing in history/social studies and in science and technical subjects. The reading standards, in particular, are intended to complement the content standards of these specific disciplines, not to replace them (NGA & CCSSO, 2010a, p. 60).

Figure I.1 provides several illustrations of how the standards in various sections and categories are connected. In each example, the Anchor Standard is provided first, followed by the grade-level expectations for one or more grades (as noted in parentheses at the end of each description).

Assessment in the CCSS

IN RECOGNIZING THE DEPTH OF THE CCSS AND the high level of expectations for students' literacy development, teachers need to monitor the pace of their instruction carefully, challenging students on a regular basis but not overwhelming them. Similarly, assessment must be ongoing without overwhelming instruction.

Assessment should be formative, thus helping teachers modify their instruction. The best formative assessment is rooted in instruction and depends on teachers being adept at gathering information from students' classroom engagement and work. Throughout this series of books, the authors provide examples of ways to assess students' readiness and learning of key content and strategies. Assessment is an area in which teacher/administrative discussions and decisions are critically important.

In addition, the requirements of the CCSS include large-scale comparative assessments to ensure that schools across the country have the same expectations of students. These assessments involve students in responding to a variety of texts and in formulating some of their responses in writing. In fact, one of the most important changes in assessment prompted by the CCSS is the use of students' written responses to measure their reading comprehension. Achieving this deeper look at students' comprehension is complicated by several pragmatic issues, such as the time and cost involved in scoring students' writing. Regardless, this approach is certainly a major part of the assessment systems being designed. Assessment systems for research (using technology) and speaking and listening are also still being developed, so these are other areas in which teachers and informal classroom assessments will continue to be important.

Using These Books to Enhance Study of the CCSS

THIS SERIES OF TEACHER RESOURCE BOOKS IS INTENDED to support teachers, teacher teams, and administrators as they look across grade levels in building CCSS-responsive instruction. As noted earlier, the CCSS expect teachers to think broadly about the impact

FIGURE I.1 ● Examples of Connections Across the CCSS

Anchor Standards for Reading

Integration of Knowledge and Ideas

Standard 7: Integrate and evaluate content presented in diverse formats and media, including visually and quantitatively, as well as in words.

- *Literature:* Compare and contrast a written story, drama, or poem to its audio, filmed, staged, or multimedia version, analyzing the effects of techniques unique to each medium (e.g., lighting, sound, color, or camera focus and angles in a film) (grade 7).
- *Informational text:* Integrate and evaluate multiple sources of information presented in different media or formats (e.g., visually, quantitatively) as well as in words in order to address a question or solve a problem (grades 11–12).

Anchor Standards for Writing

Research to Build and Present Knowledge

Standard 8: Gather relevant information from multiple print and digital sources, assess the credibility and accuracy of each source, and integrate the information while avoiding plagiarism.

- Gather relevant information from multiple print and digital sources, using search terms effectively; assess the credibility and accuracy of each source; and quote or paraphrase the data and conclusions of others while avoiding plagiarism and following a standard format for citation (grade 8).

Anchor Standards for Speaking and Listening

Presentation of Knowledge and Ideas

Standard 5: Make strategic use of digital media and visual displays of data to express information and enhance understanding of presentations.

- Make strategic use of digital media (e.g., textual, graphical, audio, visual, and interactive elements) in presentations to enhance understanding of findings, reasoning, and evidence and to add interest (grades 9–10).

of their instruction and the foundations they lay for students' future literacy development. For many teachers, meeting this expectation will be a challenge, and these books can provide guidance in several areas: adjusting instruction, adding reading and writing of informational text, creating content-rich instructional units, and assessing students in different ways.

In writing the four books in this series, the authors have been conscious of the importance of helping teachers scaffold students' learning across grade levels. The authors hope that engaging in collaborative discussions will help teachers to learn from colleagues at other levels and to think through how to create the most supportive instructional sequence and organization using content-based themes and units.

These books are not intended to be used alone; rather, teachers should read them while studying the CCSS. To begin, all teachers should download the CCSS and appendices so they are accessible and can be referred to regularly (see URLs for these materials in the References). In addition, the standards and related tools are available on several useful apps from organizations such as Mastery Connect and Learning Unlimited (again, see the References). It is also helpful to bookmark the websites for PARCC (n.d.) and SMARTER Balanced (n.d.) and then check with them periodically. In fact, so many resource sites are coming online that it is worth checking from time to time to see what might be worth reviewing. School districts, educational organizations, and state departments of education are developing instructional units and often make them available (or at least provide some of the structural components).

Much within the CCSS themselves also deserves careful analysis, study, and discussion among teachers of all grades. These efforts should lead to an identification of what is already in the curriculum and where instruction is currently aligned versus misaligned with the CCSS. Teachers must bear in mind that with the central focus on understanding texts, assessments need to be refocused, too. Specifically, schools should ask students to respond in writing to the content of the stories and articles they read so that a baseline can be developed to guide instructional decisions and the time allotted to each aspect of engagement with texts. Many states and districts have developed pilot assessments to ascertain how well their students do on tasks similar to those proposed by the two large consortia: PARCC and SMARTER Balanced. All teachers will find it useful to review the development of the assessments periodically and to compare them to the tools they use to assess their own students.

In designing this series of books, we have attempted to focus on the most important aspects of the CCSS and to provide a set of instructional strategies and tools that will help teachers adjust their instruction as needed to address these standards. Most of these strategies and tools have been tested by teachers and research studies and can therefore be used reliably, and others are variations of good instructional practices that reflect particular emphases of the CCSS. Some of these strategies and tools may seem familiar to teachers and have perhaps already been incorporated into their instructional routines. Regardless, these measures now take on added importance, because they can help align instruction with the expectations of the CCSS and the requirements of the assessments currently being developed.

It is important for teachers to develop a few strong instructional routines that allow them to observe and monitor students' growth over time. These routines should underscore the components of good reading comprehension, thereby helping students adopt them as regular reading practices. It is also important for teachers to keep students central in planning. Students should be able to see the purpose in whatever they are asked to do, and they should be involved in the assessment of their learning needs and achievements. Moreover, students' particular interests and experiences should be honored in classroom activities and other forms of engagement.

The CCSS provide an opportunity for teachers and districts to rethink the priorities, emphases, and assessments that are currently in place and to review how students are already engaged. The CCSS also challenge schools to look at the materials being used and the collaboration taking place across disciplines in the development of students' literacy. As stated in the beginning of this Introduction, the CCSS present both an opportunity and a challenge. By responding to these tasks together, we can explore new territory and find solutions to make twenty-first century learning a reality for all of our students.

REFERENCES

American College Testing (ACT). (2006). *Reading between the lines: What the ACT reveals about college readiness in reading.* Iowa City, IA: Author.

Graham, S., & Hebert, M. (2010). *Writing to read: Evidence for how writing can improve reading. A Carnegie Corporation Time to Act Report.* Washington, DC: Alliance for Excellent Education. Retrieved from http://carnegie.org/fileadmin/Media/Publications/WritingToRead_01.pdf.

Learning Unlimited. (n.d.). Learning Unlimited Common Core resources. *Learning Unlimited.* Retrieved from www.learningunlimitedllc.com/common-core.

Mastery Connect. (n.d.). Goodies. *Mastery Connect.* Retrieved from www.masteryconnect.com/learn-more/goodies.html.

National Assessment Governing Board. (2008). Reading framework for the 2009 National Assessment of Educational Progress. Washington, DC: U.S. Government Printing Office.

National Governors Association Center for Best Practices & Council of Chief State School Officers (NGA & CCSSO). (2010a). *Common Core State Standards.* Washington, DC: Authors. Retrieved from www.corestandards.org/assets/CCSSI_ELA%20Standards.pdf.

National Governors Association Center for Best Practices & Council of Chief State School Officers (NGA & CCSSO). (2010b). Appendix A, *Common Core State Standards.* Washington, DC: Authors. Retrieved from www.corestandards.org/assets/Appendix_A.pdf.

National Governors Association Center for Best Practices & Council of Chief State School Officers (NGA & CCSSO). (2010c). Appendix B, *Common Core State Standards.* Washington, DC: Authors. Retrieved from www.corestandards.org/assets/Appendix_B.pdf.

Partnership for Assessment of Readiness for College and Careers (PARCC). (n.d.). *PARCC.* Retrieved from www.parcconline.org.

SMARTER Balanced Assessment Consortium. (n.d.). Common Core State Standards Tools & Resources. *SMARTER Balanced.* Retrieved from www.smarterbalanced.org/k-12-education/common-core-state-standards-tools-resources.

Wisconsin Department of Public Instruction. (n.d.) Common Core State Standards. *Wisconsin Department of Public Instruction.* Retrieved from http://standards.dpi.wi.gov/stn_ccss.

chapter 1

The Common Core English Language Arts Standards for Grades 6–8

AS EDUCATORS, MANY OF US HAVE EXPERIENCED OPPORTUNITIES to integrate new standards into our teaching. In fact, most of us have probably had more than one experience of this type. We seem to have this experience every time new state standards are developed, but this time, the context is different. This time, we are busy integrating and implementing the Common Core State Standards, a set of expectations shared by most states and many U.S. territories.

Monkey Business/Fotolia

As we begin working with this set of Standards, we need to understand both the College and Career Readiness (CCR) Anchor Standards and the Common Core State Standards. We need to know how the Standards function and are interrelated as we align our teaching to the Common Core. We also need to know that the standards are built on an integrated model of literacy.

The goal in this chapter is to delineate the Common Core State Standards for grades 6–8. We begin by exploring the English Language Arts Standards, including the College and Career Readiness Anchor Standards and the Common Sore State Standards. Next, we discuss the language of the Common Core and the need to teach it to students. Then, we examine both formative and summative assessment and their integration in Common Core classrooms. Finally, we consider what is and what is not included in the Common Core State Standards.

The English Language Arts (ELA) Standards

THE CONNECTIONS BETWEEN THE COMMON CORE STATE STANDARDS and ELA for grades 6–8 come from two documents: *College and Career Readiness Anchor Standards for Reading, Writing, Speaking and Listening, and Language* (NGA & CCSSO, 2010c) and the *Common Core State Standards: English Language Arts and Literacy in History/Social Studies, Science, and Technical Subjects* (NGA & CCSSO, 2010d). There are College and Career Readiness Anchor Standards and Common Core State Standards for reading, writing, speaking and listening, and language. There are ten College and Career Readiness Anchor Standards for Reading, ten for Writing, six for Speaking and Listening, and six for Language. The Common Core State Standards are built upon the College and Career Readiness Anchor Standards.

In addition, three appendixes have been developed to complement the standards and provide resources we can use as we seek to understand and implement them. Appendix A provides research that supports key elements of the standards and a glossary of terms (NGA & CCSSO, 2010e). Appendix B comprises text exemplars and sample student tasks (NGA & CCSSO, 2010f), and Appendix C provides samples of student writing (NGA & CCSSO, 2010g).

In designing the Common Core State Standards, the developers focused on key considerations. The most prominent include the following

- a focus on results, rather than means
- an integrated model of literacy
- the integration of research and media skills
- shared responsibility for students' literacy development among teachers in all areas

The College and Career Readiness Anchor Standards

THE COLLEGE AND CAREER READINESS ANCHOR STANDARDS "anchor the document and define general, cross-disciplinary literacy expectations that must be met for students to be prepared to enter college and workforce training programs ready to succeed" (NGA & CCSSO, 2010d, p. 4). College- and career-ready students are described as having these qualities:

- Demonstrating independence as learners
- Building strong content knowledge
- Responding to the varying demands of audience, task, purpose, and discipline
- Comprehending as well as critiquing
- Valuing evidence
- Using technology and digital media strategically and capably
- Understanding other perspectives and cultures (NGA & CCSSO, 2010d, p. 7)

Key features of the CCR Standards include:

1. reading, with emphases on text complexity and the growth of comprehension
2. writing, with emphases on text types, responding to reading, and research
3. speaking and listening, with emphases on flexible communication and collaboration
4. language, with emphases on conventions, effective use, and vocabulary (NGA & CCSSO, 2010d, p. 8)

The College and Career Readiness Anchor Standards for Reading in grades 6–8 are organized into four clusters:

1. Key Ideas and Details
2. Craft and Structure
3. Integration of Knowledge and Ideas
4. Range of Reading and Level of Text Complexity (NGA & CCSSO, 2010d, p. 35)

The Anchor Standards address a variety of topics. For example, standards in the cluster Key Ideas and Details address close reading, themes and summarizing, and analyzing how individuals and ideas interact throughout a text. The Craft and Structure standards address word choice, text structure, and point of view. Standards in the cluster Integration of Knowledge and Ideas focus on content in diverse forms and media, reasoning and argument, and comparing and contrasting two texts. The final cluster, Range of Reading and Level of Text Complexity, addresses a single topic: comprehension of complex text.

TABLE 1.1 ● *College and Career Readiness Anchor Standards for Language*

Conventions of Standard English

1. Demonstrate command of the conventions of standard English grammar and usage when writing or speaking.
2. Demonstrate command of the conventions of standard English capitalization, punctuation, and spelling when writing.

Knowledge of Language

3. Apply knowledge of language to understand how language functions in different contexts, to make effective choices for meaning or style, and to comprehend more fully when reading or listening.

Vocabulary Acquisition and Use

4. Determine or clarify the meaning of unknown and multiple-meaning words and phrases by using context clues, analyzing meaningful word parts, and consulting general and specialized reference materials, as appropriate.
5. Demonstrate understanding of figurative language, word relationships, and nuances in word meanings.
6. Acquire and use accurately a range of general academic and domain-specific words and phrases sufficient for reading, writing, speaking, and listening at the college and career readiness level; demonstrate independence in gathering vocabulary knowledge when considering a word or phrase important to comprehension or expression.

The CCR Anchor Standards provide a foundation for the CCSS across grades K–12. In the English Language Arts, these standards address reading, writing, speaking and listening, and language. In this book, the Anchor Standards for grades 6–8 are discussed in these chapters: reading (2 and 4), writing (6), speaking and listening (5), and language (3). The College and Career Readiness Anchor Standards for Language are featured in Table 1.1.

The Common Core State Standards

ACCORDING TO THE DEVELOPERS OF THE COMMON CORE, the Standards have these key qualities:

1. Are aligned with college and work expectations;
2. Are clear, understandable, and consistent;
3. Include rigorous content and application of knowledge through high-order skills;

4. Build upon strengths and lessons of current state standards;

5. Are informed by other top performing countries, so that all students are prepared to succeed in our global economy and society; and

6. Are evidence-based. (Common Core State Standards Initiative, 2010c)

The Common Core State Standards delineate what students should know and be able to do by the end of specific grade levels. The Standards define the skills and knowledge required of all students.

Standard Strands

The Common Core State Standards are divided into four strands: Reading, Writing, Speaking and Listening, and Language. Within each area, the standards are organized according to the clusters established in the Career Readiness Anchor Standards. Some grade-level standards are similar across text types and disciplines, but others are quite different. Table 1.2 presents four variations of Reading Standard 6 for grade 8.

Reading   The Common Core State Standards for Reading are divided into two substrands—Literature and Informational Text—but both sets of standards are based on the same four clusters that appear in the College and Career Readiness Anchor Standards: (1) Key Ideas and Details, (2) Craft and Structure, (3) Integration of Knowledge and Ideas, and (4) Range of Reading and Level of Text Complexity.

The Common Core State Reading Standards for Literature address what students need to know and be able to do when reading a narrative, or story-based, text. Topics addressed within these standards across grades 6–8 are diverse. For example, Standard 1 is text based and focuses on citing evidence from text, explicit content of text, and text-based inferences.

TABLE 1.2 ● *Variations of Reading Standard 6 for Grade 8*

- **Reading Literature (Grade 8):** Analyze how differences in the points of view of the characters and the audience or reader (e.g., created through the use of dramatic irony) create such effects as suspense or humor.

- **Reading Informational Text (Grade 8):** Determine an author's point of view or purpose in a text and analyze how the author acknowledges and responds to conflicting evidence or viewpoints.

- **Literacy in History/Social Studies (Grades 6–8):** Identify aspects of a text that reveal an author's point of view or purpose (e.g., loaded language, inclusion or avoidance of particular facts).

- **Literacy in Science and Technical Subjects (Grades 6–8):** Analyze the author's purpose in providing an explanation, describing a procedure, or discussing an experiment in a text.

The primary topic of Standard 2 is determining the central idea and theme of a text. The remaining standards delineate additional text-based topics, including story elements, use of words and phrases, text structures, point of view, and text complexity. (For an overview of the content of the Common Core State Standards for Reading—Literature, structured by cluster, see Chapter 2, Table 2.2.)

The Common Core State Reading Standards for Informational Text focus on what students need to know and be able to do when reading informational or factual text. For example, in the cluster Key Ideas and Details, the focus is on topics such as citing textual evidence and determining central ideas. In the cluster Craft and Structure, word choice, structure, and point of view are among the emphases. The standards in the Integration of Knowledge and Ideas cluster focus on topics such as making arguments and specific claims and analyzing works on the same topic written by different authors. In the cluster Range of Reading and Level of Text Complexity, the sole standard addresses comprehending texts at the high end of the grades 6–8 complexity band. (For an overview of the content of the Common Core State Standards for Reading—Informational Text, structured by cluster, see Chapter 2, Table 2.3.)

Writing   The Common Core State Standards for Writing address what is required when creating specific types of text, as well as aspects of writing that are more general in nature. The clusters within this section of the Standards are (1) Text Types and Purposes, (2) Production and Distribution of Writing, (3) Research to Build and Present Knowledge, and (4) Range of Writing. In the first cluster, the three standards address three types of writing: argumentative, informational/explanatory, and narrative. In the remaining clusters, the standards address coherent writing, steps in a writing process, using technology, conducting research, and writing routinely over time. (For a more detailed view of the Writing Standards for grades 6–8, see Chapter 6.)

Speaking and Listening   The Common Core State Standards for Speaking and Listening are organized into two clusters and emphasize a range of oral communication and interpersonal skills. The standards in the cluster Comprehension and Collaboration address collaborative discussions, information presented in diverse media and formats, and evaluating arguments. The standards in the second cluster, Presentation of Knowledge and Ideas, focus on making oral presentations, integrating multimedia, and adapting speech to context and task.

Language   The Common Core State Language Standards are divided into three clusters: (1) Conventions of Standard English, (2) Knowledge of Language, and (3) Vocabulary Acquisition and Use. The first cluster includes topics such as conventional grammar and usage and conventional capitalization, punctuation, and spelling. The only standard in the second cluster, Knowledge of Language, focuses on language use in context. Among the emphases in the third cluster, Vocabulary Acquisition and Use, are strategies for determining word meanings, understanding of figurative language, and building academic vocabulary.

Understanding the Standards

To integrate the Common Core State Standards into our teaching, we must understand them. This involves reading and rereading the standards, as we "backward map" from the Anchor Standards to the strands and the grade-level standards. Of course, our efforts cannot end there!

Next, we need to read the Standards both vertically and horizontally within each strand. Reading vertically will help us to understand the breadth and depth of what our students need to know and be able to do at the end of the grade level we teach. For example, if we teach grade 8 and wanted to gain a general understanding of the Common Core State Standards for our students, we should read the grade 8 Standards vertically. Reading horizontally will help us to understand what our students need to know and be able to do before they arrive in the grade level we teach and what they need to know the following year. For example, if we are eighth-grade teachers, we should read Standards 1 through 10 horizontally from kindergarten to grade 8 to develop an understanding of what students should already know and be able to do.

A prime example of the benefit of reading horizontally can be found in the first Reading standard for Literature, in which students in grades K–3 are expected to "ask and answer questions." In the same Standard for grades 6–8, expectations focus on citing evidence from text and making inferences. The writers of the Standards have assumed that students in grades 4–8 know how to ask and answer questions, but that very well may not be the case, particularly when it comes to generating questions involving higher levels of thinking. Reading the Standards horizontally illuminates such assumptions and reminds us that there may be topics not included in our students' grade-level standards that we still need to teach.

Table 1.3 features the Common Core State Language Standards for grades 6–8. In reading this section, eighth-grade teachers can see which Standards are required for eighth grade (reading vertically) and which Standards their students should have met in the previous two years (reading horizontally).

It is important to note that when discussing or using the College and Career Readiness Anchor Standards for planning, we can identify them by strand, CCR status, and number. For example, the label *R.CCR.6* stands for Reading, College and Career Readiness, Standard 6. Similarly, individual grade-specific standards can be identified by strand, grade, and number (or number and letter, where applicable). For example, *RI.4.3* stands for Reading, Informational Text, grade 4, Standard 3 and *W.5.1a* stands for Writing, grade 5, Standard 1a (NGA & CCSSO, 2010c, p. 8).

TABLE 1.3 • Common Core State Standards for Language: Grades 6–8

Grade 6 students:	Grade 7 students:	Grade 8 students:
Conventions of Standard English		
1. Demonstrate command of the conventions of standard English grammar and usage when writing or speaking.	1. Demonstrate command of the conventions of standard English grammar and usage when writing or speaking.	1. Demonstrate command of the conventions of standard English grammar and usage when writing or speaking.
a. Ensure that pronouns are in the proper case (subjective, objective, possessive).	a. Explain the function of phrases and clauses in general and their function in specific sentences.	a. Explain the function of verbals (gerunds, participles, infinitives) in general and their function in particular sentences.
b. Use intensive pronouns (e.g., *myself, ourselves*).	b. Choose among simple, compound, complex, and compound-complex sentences to signal differing relationships among ideas.	b. Form and use verbs in the active and passive voice.
c. Recognize and correct inappropriate shifts in pronoun number and person.*	c. Place phrases and clauses within a sentence, recognizing and correcting misplaced and dangling modifiers.*	c. Form and use verbs in the indicative, imperative, interrogative, conditional, and subjunctive mood.
d. Recognize and correct vague pronouns (i.e., ones with unclear or ambiguous antecedents).*		d. Recognize and correct inappropriate shifts in verb voice and mood.*
e. Recognize variations from standard English in their own and others' writing and speaking, and identify and use strategies to improve expression in conventional language.*		

(continued)

TABLE 1.3 ● *(continued)*

Grade 6 students:	Grade 7 students:	Grade 8 students:

2. Demonstrate command of the conventions of standard English capitalization, punctuation, and spelling when writing.
 	
  a. Use punctuation (commas, parentheses, dashes) to set off nonrestrictive/parenthetical elements.*
 	
  b. Spell correctly.
	2. Demonstrate command of the conventions of standard English capitalization, punctuation, and spelling when writing.
	
	  a. Use a comma to separate coordinate adjectives (e.g., *It was a fascinating, enjoyable movie* but not *He wore an old[,] green shirt*).
	
	  b. Spell correctly.
		2. Demonstrate command of the conventions of standard English capitalization, punctuation, and spelling when writing.
		
		  a. Use punctuation (comma, ellipsis, dash) to indicate a pause or break.
		
		  b. Use an ellipsis to indicate an omission.
		
		  c. Spell correctly.

Knowledge of Language

Grade 6 students:	Grade 7 students:	Grade 8 students:

3. Use knowledge of language and its conventions when writing, speaking, reading, or listening.
 	
  a. Vary sentence patterns for meaning, reader/ listener interest, and style.*
 	
  b. Maintain consistency in style and tone.*
	3. Use knowledge of language and its conventions when writing, speaking, reading, or listening.
	
	  a. Choose language that expresses ideas precisely and concisely, recognizing and eliminating wordiness and redundancy.*
		3. Use knowledge of language and its conventions when writing, speaking, reading, or listening.
		
		  a. Use verbs in the active and passive voice and in the conditional and subjunctive mood to achieve particular effects (e.g., emphasizing the actor or the action; expressing uncertainty or describing a state contrary to fact).

*Beginning in grade 3, skills and understandings that are particularly likely to require continued attention in higher grades as they are applied to increasingly sophisticated writing and speaking are marked with an asterisk (*).

(continued)

TABLE 1.3 ● (continued)

Grade 6 students:	Grade 7 students:	Grade 8 students:
Vocabulary Acquisition and Use		
4. Determine or clarify the meaning of unknown and multiple-meaning words and phrases based on *grade 6 reading and content*, choosing flexibly from a range of strategies.	4. Determine or clarify the meaning of unknown and multiple-meaning words and phrases based on *grade 7 reading and content*, choosing flexibly from a range of strategies.	4. Determine or clarify the meaning of unknown and multiple-meaning words or phrases based on *grade 8 reading and content*, choosing flexibly from a range of strategies.
a. Use context (e.g., the overall meaning of a sentence or paragraph; a word's position or function in a sentence) as a clue to the meaning of a word or phrase.	a. Use context (e.g., the overall meaning of a sentence or paragraph; a word's position or function in a sentence) as a clue to the meaning of a word or phrase.	a. Use context (e.g., the overall meaning of a sentence or paragraph; a word's position or function in a sentence) as a clue to the meaning of a word or phrase.
b. Use common, grade-appropriate Greek or Latin affixes and roots as clues to the meaning of a word (e.g., *audience, auditory, audible*).	b. Use common, grade-appropriate Greek or Latin affixes and roots as clues to the meaning of a word (e.g., *belligerent, bellicose, rebel*).	b. Use common, grade-appropriate Greek or Latin affixes and roots as clues to the meaning of a word (e.g., *precede, recede, secede*).
c. Consult reference materials (e.g., dictionaries, glossaries, thesauruses), both print and digital, to find the pronunciation of a word or determine or clarify its precise meaning or its part of speech.	c. Consult general and specialized reference materials (e.g., dictionaries, glossaries, thesauruses), both print and digital, to find the pronunciation of a word or determine or clarify its precise meaning or its part of speech.	c. Consult general and specialized reference materials (e.g., dictionaries, glossaries, thesauruses), both print and digital, to find the pronunciation of a word or determine or clarify its precise meaning or its part of speech.
d. Verify the preliminary determination of the meaning of a word or phrase (e.g., by checking the inferred meaning in context or in a dictionary).	d. Verify the preliminary determination of the meaning of a word or phrase (e.g., by checking the inferred meaning in context or in a dictionary).	d. Verify the preliminary determination of the meaning of a word or phrase (e.g., by checking the inferred meaning in context or in a dictionary).

(continued)

TABLE 1.3 ● *(continued)*

Grade 6 students:	Grade 7 students:	Grade 8 students:
5. Demonstrate understanding of figurative language, word relationships, and nuances in word meanings.	5. Demonstrate understanding of figurative language, word relationships, and nuances in word meanings.	5. Demonstrate understanding of figurative language, word relationships, and nuances in word meanings.
a. Interpret figures of speech (e.g., personification) in context.	a. Interpret figures of speech (e.g., literary, biblical, and mythological allusions) in context.	a. Interpret figures of speech (e.g. verbal irony, puns) in context.
b. Use the relationship between particular words (e.g., cause/effect, part/whole, item/category) to better understand each of the words.	b. Use the relationship between particular words (e.g., synonym/antonym, analogy) to better understand each of the words.	b. Use the relationship between particular words to better understand each of the words.
c. Distinguish among the connotations (associations) of words with similar denotations (definitions) (e.g., *stingy, scrimping, economical, unwasteful, thrifty*).	c. Distinguish among the connotations (associations) of words with similar denotations (definitions) (e.g., *refined, respectful, polite, diplomatic, condescending*).	c. Distinguish among the connotations (associations) of words with similar denotations (definitions) (e.g., *bullheaded, willful, firm, persistent, resolute*).
6. Acquire and use accurately grade-appropriate general academic and domain-specific words and phrases; gather vocabulary knowledge when considering a word or phrase important to comprehension or expression.	6. Acquire and use accurately grade-appropriate general academic and domain-specific words and phrases; gather vocabulary knowledge when considering a word or phrase important to comprehension or expression.	6. Acquire and use accurately grade-appropriate general academic and domain-specific words and phrases; gather vocabulary knowledge when considering a word or phrase important to comprehension or expression.

(continued)

The Language of the Standards

A NUMBER OF TERMS APPEAR FREQUENTLY in both the College and Career Readiness Anchor Standards and the Common Core State Standards. Typically, they are verbs used to describe student expectations. Among the verbs employed are *determine, analyze, compare and contrast, cite, trace, delineate,* and *evaluate.*

From a teaching standpoint, we need to ensure that students understand these terms so they can fully understand the expectations of the Standards. For example, the word *analyze* is used quite frequently. In the College and Career Readiness Anchor Standards, students are expected to *analyze* how and why people and ideas develop and interact, how texts are structured, and how two or more texts address similar themes or topics. In the Common Core State Standards for Reading Literature, students' ability to *analyze* is the expectation of Standards 3, 5, and 6, and for Reading Informational Text, it is the ability to *analyze* Standards 3, 5, and 9.

Most definitions of *analyze* focus on examining the structure of information in detail, particularly for the purpose of explanation. *Analyzing* requires responding in a way that demonstrates an ability to see patterns and to classify information into groups or parts. As teachers, we may also be familiar with the term *analyze* as a level in Bloom's taxonomy, in which it is defined as taking something learned apart to think about the parts and how they fit together (Bloom, 2013). For example, when analyzing informational text, our students must be able to use several skills—principal among them are the abilities to generate and respond to questions and to use text structures. Both of these skills contribute to readers' comprehension. We need to teach our students these skills as we prepare them to engage in analysis (McLaughlin & Fisher, 2012/2013).

Asking and answering questions and understanding text structures are Common Core expectations in the lower grades but not in grades 6–8. Because all students need to have these valuable skills, we need teach our students how to use them—to think actively about what they are learning. This is the foundation of *analysis,* a level of thinking in which all students in grades 6–8 need to successfully engage.

Assessment in the Common Core Classroom

CLASSROOM ASSESSMENT IS TYPICALLY FORMATIVE OR SUMMATIVE in nature. Formative assessment is used every day; summative assessment is used periodically.

Formative assessment captures students' performance as they engage in the process of learning. This type of assessment affords insights into students' understandings at any point in the learning experience. Formative assessment does not involve quizzes and tests. Rather, it reflects constructivist theory and is viewed not as an add-on but as a natural component of teaching and learning.

Both students and teachers take active roles in formative assessment, which is typically informal in nature and can be used in a variety of instructional settings. This includes scaffolded learning experiences, in which students are provided with varying degrees of teacher support. In this context, assessment captures students' emerging abilities and provides insights that may not be gleaned from independent settings (Minick, 1987). Examples of formative assessments include strategy applications such as Bookmark Technique (McLaughlin, 2010), the Concept of Definition Map (Schwartz & Raphael, 1986), and KWL (Ogle, 1986). Observations, discussion, and informal writing are among the numerous other possibilities.

Formative assessment presents a natural, viable, and continuous means for teachers to learn about what students know and can do. It is a natural component of everyday teaching and provides insightful information about students and the learning process. Formative assessment is distinctive because it documents the responsiveness of the learner not only during initial teaching, but also during subsequent instruction that has been designed in response to the learner's needs. Formative assessment can easily be incorporated in grade 6–8 Common Core classrooms.

In 2013, the International Reading Association published a Position Statement on Formative Assessment (IRA, 2013). In this statement, *formative assessment* is defined as "a purposeful process that provides teachers and students with descriptive feedback concerning students' literacy" (p. 1). The full text of the position statement provides general information about formative assessment and makes recommendations for policy and practice. As stated in this document, "The International Reading Association believes that using formative assessment in accordance with the appropriate principles, practices, and recommendations will contribute considerably to student literacy achievement and personal growth" (p. 3).

In classrooms, summative assessment is typically used at the ends of units or embedded in long-term projects. Summative assessment typically involves the use of rubrics. State assessments, school district assessments, end-of-unit assessments, and, indeed, the Common Core-commissioned assessments are other examples of summative assessments.

What Is and Is Not Included in the CCSS

THE AUTHORS OF THE COMMON CORE STATE THAT "the Standards should be recognized for what they are not as well as what they are" (NGA & CCSSO, 2010d, p. 6). In this section, we briefly review what is addressed in the Common Core, and what is missing in relation to literacy.

To begin, both our teaching and the Standards are based on integrated language arts models. The following parallels can be drawn:

- **Reading comprehension:** Although the Common Core State Standards do not address reading comprehension strategies in any significant way, they do address aspects of comprehension, including making inferences, understanding text structures, and developing vocabulary.

- **Vocabulary:** Vocabulary is addressed in the Common Core State Standards across multiple strands, including Language, Reading, and Writing.
- **Writing:** The Writing Standards address this specific language art in depth, covering a variety of types of writing and integrating the use of technology.
- **Discussion:** Discussion skills are addressed in the Speaking and Listening standards, which comprise an entire strand of the Common Core State Standards.

Although the Common Core State Standards focus on what students are expected to know and be able to do, "they do not describe all that can or should be taught" (NGA & CCSSO, 2010d, p. 6). The authors of the Standards make this point in the introduction to the document. They further note that although the Standards delineate expectations for students, they leave a great deal of decision making to the discretion of teachers and curriculum developers. Essentially, the Common Core Initiative has provided the Standards, but the teaching has been left in the hands of the educators. For example, as stated in the Common Core State Standards document:

> The Standards do not mandate such things as a particular writing process or the full range of metacognitive strategies that students may need to monitor and direct their thinking and learning. Teachers are thus free to provide students with whatever tools and knowledge their professional judgment and experience identify as most helpful for meeting the goals set out in the Standards. (NGA & CCSSO, 2010d, p. 4)

In addition, the Common Core State Standards do not include advanced work for students who meet the Standards before completing high school, nor do they delineate the methods or materials needed to support students who are significantly above or below grade-level expectations. "No set of grade-specific standards can fully reflect the great variety in abilities, needs, learning rates, and achievement levels of students in any given classroom" (NGA & CCSSO, 2010d, p. 6).

Although the Common Core State Standards do not address the types of support needed by English learners (ELLs) and students with disabilities, the authors of the Standards state that both groups of students should have a high-quality education. In a document entitled *Application of the Common Core State Standards for English Language Learners* (NGA & CCSSO, 2010a), the creators of the Standards note that for English learners to meet the Common Core State Standards, they need access to the following:

- Teachers and personnel at the school and district levels who are well prepared and qualified to support ELLs while taking advantage of the many strengths and skills they bring to the classroom;
- Literacy-rich school environments where students are immersed in a variety of language experiences;

- Instruction that develops foundational skills in English and enables ELLs to participate fully in grade-level coursework;

- Coursework that prepares ELLs for postsecondary education or the workplace, yet is made comprehensible for students learning content in a second language (through specific pedagogical techniques and additional resources);

- Opportunities for classroom discourse and interaction that are well-designed to enable ELLs to develop communicative strengths in language arts;

- Ongoing assessment and feedback to guide learning; and

- Speakers of English who know the language well enough to provide ELLs with models and support. (pp. 1–2)

In another Common Core State Standards document, *Application to Students with Disabilities* (NGA & CCSSO, 2010b), the creators of the Standards note that students with disabilities "must be challenged to excel within the general curriculum and prepared for success in their post-school lives, including college and/or careers" (n.p.). The creators further recommend that three types of supports and services be provided for students with disabilities:

1. instructional supports for learning that are based on the principles of Universal Design for Learning (UDL)

2. instructional accommodations that allow suitable changes in materials or procedures but not in the standards

3. assistive technology devices and services that ensure students have access to the general curriculum and to the Common Core State Standards (n.p.)

It is important to remember that the Common Core State Standards are different from other standards with which we have previously taught. These distinctions occur on multiple levels. For example, adoption of the Common Core State Standards marks the first time that so many states and territories are supporting the same standards. In the past, not only did each state or territory have its own standards, but each entity also frequently wrote its own standards. The CCSS have been written by diverse panels of educators.

Other differences are evident in how the authors of the Common Core State Standards have treated particular topics. For example, Pearson and Hiebert (2012) have noted four areas in which the treatment by CCSS writers is either new or unique compared to the treatments by most previous standards documents of states or national organizations: (1) close/critical reading, (2) connections across language arts and between language arts and disciplines, (3) integration of research and media, and (4) text complexity. All four of these topics are prevalent in the grade 6–8 ELA Standards.

REFERENCES

Bloom, B. (2013). Bloom's taxonomy. Retrieved from www.bloomstaxonomy.org.

International Reading Association (IRA). (2013). *Formative assessment: A position statement of the International Reading Association.* Newark, DE: Author. Retrieved from www.reading.org/Libraries/position-statements-and-resolutions/ps1080_formative_assessment_web.pdf.

McLaughlin, M. (2010). *Content area reading: Teaching and learning in an age of multiple literacies.* Boston, MA: Allyn & Bacon.

McLaughlin, M., & Fisher, D. (2012/2013). Teaching students to meet the Common Core in grades 6–12? Analyze this! *Reading Today, 30*(3), 12–13.

Minick, N. (1987). Implications of Vygotsky's theories for dynamic assessment. In C. S. Lidz (Ed.) *Dynamic assessment: An interactional approach for evaluating learning potential* (pp. 116–140). New York: Guilford.

National Governors Association Center for Best Practices & Council of Chief State School Officers (NGA & CCSSO). (2010a). *Application of the Common Core State Standards for English language learners.* Retrieved from www.corestandards.org/assets/application-for-english-learners.pdf.

National Governors Association Center for Best Practices & Council of Chief State School Officers (NGA & CCSSO). (2010b). *Application to students with disabilities.* Retrieved from www.corestandards.org/assets/application-to-students-with-disabilities.pdf.

National Governors Association Center for Best Practices & Council of Chief State School Officers (NGA & CCSSO). (2010c). *College and Career Readiness Anchor Standards for Reading, Writing, Speaking and Listening, and Language.* Washington, DC: Authors. Retrieved from www.corestandards.org/ELA-Literacy/CCRA/R.

National Governors Association Center for Best Practices & Council of Chief State School Officers (NGA & CCSSO). (2010d). *Common Core State Standards: English Language Arts and Literacy in History/Social Studies, Science, and Technical Subjects.* Washington, DC: Authors. Retrieved from www.corestandards.org/assets/CCSSI_ELA%20Standards.pdf.

National Governors Association Center for Best Practices & Council of Chief State School Officers (NGA & CCSSO). (2010e). Appendix A: Research supporting key elements of the standards and glossary of key terms. *Common Core State Standards.* Washington, DC: Authors. Retrieved from www.corestandards.org/assets/Appendix_A.pdf.

National Governors Association Center for Best Practices & Council of Chief State School Officers (NGA & CCSSO). (2010f). Appendix B: Text exemplars and sample performance tasks. *Common Core State Standards.* Washington, DC: Authors. Retrieved from www.corestandards.org/assets/Appendix_B.pdf.

National Governors Association Center for Best Practices & Council of Chief State School Officers (NGA & CCSSO). (2010g). Appendix C: Samples of student writing. *Common Core State Standards.* Washington, DC: Authors. Retrieved from www.corestandards.org/assets/Appendix_C.pdf.

Ogle, D. (1986). K-W-L: A teaching model that develops active reading of expository text. *The Reading Teacher, 39,* 564–570.

Pearson, P. D., & Hiebert, E. H. (2012). Understanding the Common Core State Standards. In L. M. Morrow, T. Shanahan, & K. K. Wixson (Eds.), *Teaching with the Common Core Standards for English Language Arts, PreK–2.* New York, NY: Guilford Press.

Schwartz, R., & Raphael, T. (1985). Concept of definition: A key to improving students' vocabulary. *The Reading Teacher, 39*(2), 198–205.

Reading Comprehension

WHEN WE THINK ABOUT WHAT OUR STUDENTS NEED to know to be successful in meeting the Common Core Reading Standards (CCSS), we need to understand what the Standards entail. In addition, we need to know what the teaching of reading requires. The reality is that not everything students need to know about reading is included in the CCSS. As noted in Chapter 1, the writers of the CCSS created the Standards, but they left the teaching in our hands.

The purpose of this chapter is to situate the Common Core State Standards within the research, theory, and practice involved in the teaching of reading. To that end, we examine not only the CCSS Reading standards but also what students need to know and be able to do in reading to meet the Standards successfully.

This chapter is divided into four sections. First, we delineate what the Common Core has to say about reading, emphasizing specific connections such as narrative and informational

Annie Pickert Fuller/Pearson

text structures. Next, we examine what we know about reading, placing special emphasis on reading comprehension. Then we explore examples of CCSS-based rich instructional tasks, including classroom examples of teaching ideas that support reading, as it is addressed in the Common Core State Standards. Finally, we consider *Inside the Common Core Classroom,* a vignette of one classroom teacher's choices when teaching to the Common Core.

The Common Core Reading Standards

THE COLLEGE AND CAREER READINESS (CCR) Anchor Standards are the broad statements that serve as the foundation of the CCSS for grades 6–12. There are 10 CCR College and Career Readiness Anchor Standards for Reading ranging in topic from reading closely to analyzing text structures to reading complex text. The complete list of Anchor Standards for Reading is presented in Table 2.1.

TABLE 2.1 ● *College and Career Readiness Anchor Standards for Reading*

Key Ideas and Details

1. Read closely to determine what the text says explicitly and to make logical inferences from it; cite specific textual evidence when writing or speaking to support conclusions drawn from the text.
2. Determine central ideas or themes of a text and analyze their development; summarize the key supporting details and ideas.
3. Analyze how and why individuals, events, and ideas develop and interact over the course of a text.

Craft and Structure

4. Interpret words and phrases as they are used in a text, including determining technical, connotative, and figurative meanings, and analyze how specific word choices shape meaning or tone.
5. Analyze the structure of texts, including how specific sentences, paragraphs, and larger portions of the text (e.g., a section, chapter, scene, or stanza) relate to each other and the whole.
6. Assess how point of view or purpose shapes the content and style of a text.

Integration of Knowledge and Ideas

7. Integrate and evaluate content presented in diverse formats and media, including visually and quantitatively, as well as in words.*
8. Delineate and evaluate the argument and specific claims in a text, including the validity of the reasoning as well as the relevance and sufficiency of the evidence.
9. Analyze how two or more texts address similar themes or topics in order to build knowledge or to compare the approaches the authors take.

Range of Reading and Level of Text Complexity

10. Read and comprehend complex literary and informational texts independently and proficiently.

*Please see "Research to Build Knowledge" in Writing and "Comprehension and Collaboration" in Speaking and Listening for additional standards relevant to gathering, assigning, and applying information from print and digital sources.

The Common Core State Standards for Reading are divided into two substrands: Literature and Informational Text (NGA & CCSSO, 2010). Some concepts are addressed in both areas, but others are unique to one or the other. For example, the concept *point of view* is an emphasis in both the Literature Standards and the Informational Text Standards. Conversely, the concept *multimedia* is barely mentioned in the Literature standards in the cluster Integration of Knowledge and Ideas, but it is prevalent in the same cluster of the Informational Text Standards. The CCSS Reading standards for Literature (Standards 1–10) are provided in Table 2.2, and the CCSS Reading standards for Informational Text (Standards 1–10) are provided in Table 2.3. Both tables feature the standards for grades 6–8.

TABLE 2.2 ● *Common Core State Standards for Reading Literature, Grades 6–8*

Grade 6 Students:	Grade 7 Students:	Grade 8 Students:
Key Ideas and Details		
1. Cite textual evidence to support analysis of what the text says explicitly as well as inferences drawn from the text.	1. Cite several pieces of textual evidence to support analysis of what the text says explicitly as well as inferences drawn from the text.	1. Cite the textual evidence that most strongly supports an analysis of what the text says explicitly as well as inferences drawn from the text.
2. Determine a theme or central idea of a text and how it is conveyed through particular details; provide a summary of the text distinct from personal opinions or judgments.	2. Determine a theme or central idea of a text and analyze its development over the course of the text; provide an objective summary of the text.	2. Determine a theme or central idea of a text and analyze its development over the course of the text, including its relationship to the characters, setting, and plot; provide an objective summary of the text.
3. Describe how a particular story's or drama's plot unfolds in a series of episodes as well as how the characters respond or change as the plot moves toward a resolution.	3. Analyze how particular elements of a story or drama interact (e.g., how setting shapes the characters or plot).	3. Analyze how particular lines of dialogue or incidents in a story or drama propel the action, reveal aspects of a character, or provoke a decision.
Craft and Structure		
4. Determine the meaning of words and phrases as they are used in a text, including figurative and connotative meanings; analyze the impact of a specific word choice on meaning and tone.	4. Determine the meaning of words and phrases as they are used in a text, including figurative and connotative meanings; analyze the impact of rhymes and other repetitions of sounds (e.g., alliteration) on a specific verse or stanza of a poem or section of a story or drama.	4. Determine the meaning of words and phrases as they are used in a text, including figurative and connotative meanings; analyze the impact of specific word choices on meaning and tone, including analogies or allusions to other texts.

(continued)

TABLE 2.2 ● *(continued)*

Craft and Structure (continued)		
5. Analyze how a particular sentence, chapter, scene, or stanza fits into the overall structure of a text and contributes to the development of the theme, setting, or plot.	5. Analyze how a drama's or poem's form or structure (e.g., soliloquy, sonnet) contributes to its meaning.	5. Compare and contrast the structure of two or more texts and analyze how the differing structure of each text contributes to its meaning and style.
6. Explain how an author develops the point of view of the narrator or speaker in a text.	6. Analyze how an author develops and contrasts the points of view of different characters or narrators in a text.	6. Analyze how differences in the points of view of the characters and the audience or reader (e.g., created through the use of dramatic irony) create such effects as suspense or humor.

TABLE 2.3 ● *Common Core State Standards for Reading Informational Text, Grades 6–12*

Grade 6 Students:	Grade 7 Students:	Grade 8 Students:
Key Ideas and Details		
1. Cite textual evidence to support analysis of what the text says explicitly as well as inferences drawn from the text.	1. Cite several pieces of textual evidence to support analysis of what the text says explicitly as well as inferences drawn from the text.	1. Cite the textual evidence that most strongly supports an analysis of what the text says explicitly as well as inferences drawn from the text.
2. Determine a central idea of a text and how it is conveyed through particular details; provide a summary of the text distinct from personal opinions or judgments.	2. Determine two or more central ideas in a text and analyze their development over the course of the text; provide an objective summary of the text.	2. Determine a central idea of a text and analyze its development over the course of the text, including its relationship to supporting ideas; provide an objective summary of the text.
3. Analyze in detail how a key individual, event, or idea is introduced, illustrated, and elaborated in a text (e.g., through examples or anecdotes).	3. Analyze the interactions between individuals, events, and ideas in a text (e.g., how ideas influence individuals or events, or how individuals influence ideas or events).	3. Analyze how a text makes connections among and distinctions between individuals, ideas, or events (e.g., through comparisons, analogies, or categories).

(continued)

TABLE 2.3 ● *(continued)*

Craft and Structure

4. Determine the meaning of words and phrases as they are used in a text, including figurative, connotative, and technical meanings.

4. Determine the meaning of words and phrases as they are used in a text, including figurative, connotative, and technical meanings; analyze the impact of a specific word choice on meaning and tone.

4. Determine the meaning of words and phrases as they are used in a text, including figurative, connotative, and technical meanings; analyze the impact of specific word choices on meaning and tone, including analogies or allusions to other texts.

5. Analyze how a particular sentence, paragraph, chapter, or section fits into the overall structure of a text and contributes to the development of the ideas.

5. Analyze the structure an author uses to organize a text, including how the major sections contribute to the whole and to the development of the ideas.

5. Analyze in detail the structure of a specific paragraph in a text, including the role of particular sentences in developing and refining a key concept.

6. Determine an author's point of view or purpose in a text and explain how it is conveyed in the text.

6. Determine an author's point of view or purpose in a text and analyze how the author distinguishes his or her position from that of others.

6. Determine an author's point of view or purpose in a text and analyze how the author acknowledges and responds to conflicting evidence or viewpoints.

Integration of Knowledge and Ideas

7. Integrate information presented in different media or formats (e.g., visually, quantitatively) as well as in words to develop a coherent understanding of a topic or issue.

7. Compare and contrast a text to an audio, video, or multimedia version of the text, analyzing each medium's portrayal of the subject (e.g., how the delivery of a speech affects the impact of the words).

7. Evaluate the advantages and disadvantages of using different mediums (e.g., print or digital text, video, multimedia) to present a particular topic or idea.

8. Trace and evaluate the argument and specific claims in a text, distinguishing claims that are supported by reasons and evidence from claims that are not.

8. Trace and evaluate the argument and specific claims in a text, assessing whether the reasoning is sound and the evidence is relevant and sufficient to support the claims.

8. Delineate and evaluate the argument and specific claims in a text, assessing whether the reasoning is sound and the evidence is relevant and sufficient; recognize when irrelevant evidence is introduced.

(continued)

TABLE 2.3 ● *(continued)*

Integration of Knowledge and Ideas (continued)		
9. Compare and contrast one author's presentation of events with that of another (e.g., a memoir written by and a biography on the same person).	9. Analyze how two or more authors writing about the same topic shape their presentations of key information by emphasizing different evidence or advancing different interpretations of facts.	9. Analyze a case in which two or more texts provide conflicting information on the same topic and identify where the texts disagree on matters of fact or interpretation.

Range of Reading and Level of Text Complexity		
10. By the end of the year, read and comprehend literary nonfiction in the grades 6–8 text complexity band proficiently, with scaffolding as needed at the high end of the range.	10. By the end of the year, read and comprehend literary nonfiction in the grades 6–8 text complexity band proficiently, with scaffolding as needed at the high end of the range.	10. By the end of the year, read and comprehend literary nonfiction at the high end of the grades 6–8 text complexity band independently and proficiently.

The Reading standards address a variety of aspects of reading, but as noted in the introduction to the CCSS, they do not address methods of teaching reading (NGA & CCSSO, 2010). For example, Standard 10 in both the CCSS Reading Standards for Literature and for Informational Text states the expectation that students will read complex text, but how to teach students to comprehend complex text is left in teachers' hands. (For more detailed information about text complexity, see Chapter 4.)

What We Know about Teaching Reading

AS LITERACY EDUCATORS, OUR COMMON GOAL IS to teach students to become active, strategic readers who can successfully comprehend text. Of course, to teach students to be successful readers, we need to know what comprehension is, as well as it how it works and how we can help our students understand what they read. Teaching students how to comprehend is particularly critical for teachers of students in grades 4–12. As noted in *Reading Next,* a report on literacy among middle school and high school students:

> Approximately eight million young people between fourth and twelfth grade struggle to read at grade level. Some 70 percent of older readers require some form of remediation. Very few of these older struggling readers need help to read the words on a page; their most common problem is that they are not able to comprehend what they read. (Biancarosa & Snow, 2006, p. 3)

There are ten essential principles that underpin effectively teaching students how to comprehend text:

1. beginning with a social constructivist view of reading;
2. understanding students' roles in the reading process;
3. being an influential teacher;
4. motivating and engaging students;
5. teaching reading comprehension strategies;
6. using differentiated instruction;
7. providing various types and levels of text;
8. encouraging students to use multiple forms of representing thinking;
9. teaching in meaningful contexts;
10. teaching students to comprehend at deeper levels. (McLaughlin, 2012, pp. 432–438)

Details of these principles follow later in this chapter. Next, we examine the research base for reading comprehension and make connections from theory to practice.

The Nature of Reading Comprehension

Today, reading researchers suggest that reading comprehension is a multifaceted process. Factors such as constructivist beliefs, influential teachers, active readers, type and nature of text, and type of instruction play important roles in the construction of meaning. This approach is markedly different from that of the 1970s, when Dolores Durkin (1978/1979) reported that little if any comprehension instruction occurred in classrooms.

In current thinking, reading comprehension is a social constructivist process that results in the personal construction of meaning. Prior knowledge is a significant factor in this process. The more prior knowledge a reader has about a given topic, the greater the possibility the reader will be able to comprehend text related to that topic. Essentially, meaning is constructed when readers make connections between what they know (prior knowledge) and what they are reading (the text).

In reading comprehension, constructivism is reflected in schema-based learning development, which suggests that learning takes place when new information is integrated with what is already known. The more prior knowledge and experience readers have with a particular topic, the easier they can make connections between what they are learning and what they know (Anderson, 2004; Anderson & Pearson, 1984). The social constructivist nature of comprehension suggests that readers refine their understanding by negotiating meaning with others. This typically occurs through discussion. Engaging students in discussion promotes active engagement in constructing meaning from a text (McKeown, Beck, & Blake, 2009). The social nature of constructing meaning also reflects Lev Vygotsky's (1978) principle of social mediation.

The Roles of Teachers and Students

Both students and teachers need to take active roles in reading. The research refers to such students as "good readers" and such educators as "influential teachers."

Much of what we know about comprehension is based on studies of good readers. These students actively participate in reading. They have clear goals and constantly monitor the relation between the goals they have set and the text they are reading (Duke & Pearson, 2002; Pressley, 2000). These readers use a repertoire of comprehension strategies to facilitate the construction of meaning. Researchers believe that using such strategies helps students become metacognitive readers, who can think about and monitor their own thinking while reading (Palincsar & Brown, 1984; Roehler & Duffy, 1984). Good readers read both narrative and informational texts and know how to figure out unfamiliar words. They use their knowledge of text structure to process text efficiently and strategically (Goldman & Rakestraw, 2000). These readers also generate questions spontaneously at different points for a variety of reasons. They are problem solvers who have the ability to discover new information on their own.

Good readers read widely, monitor their understanding, and negotiate meaning. They know when they are constructing meaning and when they are not. When comprehension breaks down due to lack of background information, difficulty of words, or unfamiliar text structure, good readers know and use a variety of "fix-up" strategies, such as rereading, changing the pace of reading, using context clues, and cross-checking cueing systems. These readers are able to select the appropriate strategies and to focus consistently on making sense of text.

Influential teachers are highly valued participants in the reading process. They know the importance of every student being able to comprehend text successfully. In fact, the International Reading Association (2000) reports that it is the teacher's knowledge that makes a difference in student achievement. The teacher's role in the reading process is to create experiences and environments that introduce, nurture, or extend students' abilities to engage with text. Doing this requires that teachers use explicit instruction, which includes modeling, scaffolding, facilitating, and participating (Au & Raphael, 1998).

Both reading researchers and professional organizations have delineated the characteristics of influential reading teachers (IRA, 2000; Ruddell, 1995, 2004):

Influential reading teachers:

- Believe that all students can learn.
- Differentiate instruction and recognize that providing motivation and offering multiple kinds of text are essential elements of teaching and learning.
- Understand that reading is a social constructivist process that functions best in authentic situations.
- Teach in print-rich, concept-rich environments.

- Have in-depth knowledge of various aspects of literacy, including both reading and writing.

- Provide myriad opportunities for students to read, write, and discuss.

- Teach for a variety of purposes, using diverse methods, materials, and grouping patterns to focus on individual students' needs, interests, and learning styles.

- Understand the skills and strategies that good readers use and can teach students how to use them.

- Continually monitor students' learning and adjust teaching as needed to ensure that all learners are successful (McLaughlin, 2012).

Emphases of Effective Teachers of Reading

Duke and Pearson (2002) describe reading comprehension as "a consuming, continuous, and complex activity, but one that, for good readers, is both satisfying and productive" (p. 206). Effective teachers also view comprehension as a complex process. To ensure their instruction is effective, they integrate such components as motivation and engagement, comprehension strategies, differentiated instruction, a range of texts at a diversity of levels, multiple representations of thinking, formative and summative assessment, meaningful contexts, and comprehending at deeper levels.

Motivation and Engagement   Motivation and engagement are key factors in comprehension. Gambrell (2011a) suggests that students who are highly motivated to read will choose to read and continue to read over time. Gambrell (1996) also suggests that "classroom cultures that foster reading motivation are characterized by a teacher who is a reading model, a book-rich classroom environment, opportunities for choice, familiarity with books, and literacy-related incentives that reflect the value of reading" (p. 20). Gambrell, Palmer, Codling, and Mazzoni (1996) note that highly motivated readers read for a wide variety of reasons, including curiosity, involvement, social interchange, and emotional satisfaction.

The *engagement perspective* on reading integrates cognitive, motivational, and social aspects of reading (Baker, Afflerbach, & Reinking, 1996; Baker & Wigfield, 1999; Guthrie & Alvermann, 1999). Engaged learners achieve because they want to understand, have intrinsic motivations for interacting with text, use cognitive skills to understand, and share their knowledge by talking with teachers and peers (Guthrie & Wigfield, 1997). Engaged readers read widely for enjoyment and have positive attitudes about reading.

Engaged readers transact with print and construct understanding based on connections between prior knowledge and new information. As described by Baker and Wigfield (1999), "Engaged readers are motivated to read for different purposes, utilize knowledge gained from previous experience to generate new understandings, and participate in meaningful social interactions around reading" (p. 453). Guthrie and Humenick (2004) suggest that having goals for reading, interest in the topic, and choices about what to read and how to respond to reading all contribute to readers' motivation and engagement.

Gambrell (2011b) has created the "Seven Rules of Engagement" for students. According to these "rules," students are more motivated to read under the following conditions:

1. The reading tasks and activities are relevant to their lives.
2. They have access to a wide range of reading materials.
3. They have ample opportunities to engage in sustained reading.
4. They have opportunities to make choices about what they read and how they engage in and complete literacy tasks.
5. They have opportunities to socially interact with others about the text they are reading.
6. They have opportunities to be successful with challenging texts.
7. Classroom incentives reflect the value and importance of reading. (pp. 173–176)

Comprehension Strategies   Pearson (2001b) has identified the three most important things we have learned about comprehension in the past 30 years:

1. Students benefit from learning and using comprehension strategies and routines.
2. Students need to have opportunities to read, write, and talk.
3. Having background knowledge supports comprehension by providing a starting point: where readers are and what they know.

Other researchers have confirmed that using a repertoire of reading comprehension strategies enhances readers' reasoning (Duke, Pressley, & Hilden, 2004; Paris & Paris, 2007; Pressley, 2006).

The terms used to identify comprehension strategies vary, to some degree, by researcher and publication, but an example of a typical set of strategies are those taught in the Guided Comprehension approach. *Guided Comprehension* provides a context in which students learn and employ comprehension strategies in a variety of settings using multiple levels and types of text (McLaughlin & Allen, 2009). The strategies taught in Guided Comprehension include the following:

- **Previewing:** Activating prior knowledge, making predictions, and setting purposes
- **Self-questioning:** Generating questions to guide reading
- **Making connections:** Relating reading to oneself, the text, and others
- **Visualizing:** Creating mental pictures of the text while reading
- **Knowing how words work:** Understanding words through strategic vocabulary development, including use of the graphophonic, syntactic, and semantic cueing systems to figure out unknown words

- **Monitoring:** Asking "Does this make sense?" while reading and adapting strategic processes as needed based on the response
- **Summarizing:** Synthesizing the important ideas of a text
- **Evaluating:** Making judgments about the content of the text and the author's craft in writing it

Research supports the idea that the explicit instruction of comprehension strategies increases students' comprehension (Duke & Pearson, 2002). Research further suggests that reading comprehension strategy instruction should begin in the primary grades (Hilden & Pressley, 2002; McLaughlin, 2003).

Explicit instruction involves directly teaching students comprehension strategies, often through a multistep process that promotes scaffolding. When we scaffold instruction, we gradually release responsibility to the students. When we use explicit instruction, we introduce the text and encourage students to activate their prior knowledge, make connections, and set purposes for reading.

McLaughlin and Allen (2009) recommend a framework for explicit strategy instruction that involves five steps: (1) explain, (2) demonstrate, (3) guide, (4) practice, and (5) reflect. For example, when teaching students to summarize, we may begin by explaining and demonstrating summarizing. In the explanation step, we define and discuss the strategies and an example application. In this case, a Sketch-and-Label Retelling could be the strategy application. In the demonstration step, we might use a think-aloud (Davey, 1983) to share our own thought processes while we model the strategy. At this point, we would provide full support to students. In the third step, we may guide students as they summarize in small groups or with partners. In this stage, we offer support as needed. Next, we encourage students to practice summarizing independently. At this point, we provide little or no support. Finally, we encourage students to reflect on what they have learned and how to use the strategy when reading other texts.

As we move from full support to providing support as needed to providing little or no support, students take on more and more responsibility. As Pearson and Hoffman (2011) note:

> Teachers who teach reading in this way are using what we have come to call the *gradual release of responsibility* (from teacher to student) for helping readers become independent and self-sufficient readers—readers who know when and whether they have understood a text, and, if they haven't, what to do to fix things. (pp. 32–33)

During explicit instruction, the teacher purposefully interacts with students and takes an active role in their acquisition of strategies by explaining, demonstrating, and guiding (Dahl & Farnan, 1998; McLaughlin, 2010a, 2010b; Roehler & Duffy, 1984). Providing explicit instruction in comprehension strategies affords the teacher opportunities to observe students in various stages of learning. As they observe students gaining competence in using strategies, the teacher gradually releases responsibility for learning to the students, who apply the strategies independently in their everyday reading after having practiced them in a variety of settings. Observing students' strategy use provides further insights into students' progress, interests, and abilities, which can often be used to differentiate additional instruction.

Differentiated Instruction   Duke and Pearson's (2002) work reminds us that learners need different kinds and amounts of reading comprehension. As teachers, we understand this. We know that we have students of differing capabilities in our classes, and we strive to help them comprehend to the best of their abilities. When we differentiate instruction, we accommodate the diversity of students' needs (Gibson & Hasbrouck, 2008; Tyner & Green, 2009).

To develop a learning environment that promotes differentiated instruction, Gibson and Hasbrouck (2008) suggest that we do the following:

- Adopt a collaborative approach to teaching and learning.
- Provide explicit instruction in both whole-class and small-group settings.
- Establish and follow routines and procedures.
- Scaffold students' learning.
- Increase students' engagement in learning.
- Teach students both how to learn and what to learn.
- Change how teaching occurs

We can differentiate key instructional elements to support students as they gain competence and confidence in learning. These include (1) the *content,* or the information being taught; (2) the *process,* or the way the information is taught; and (3) the *product,* or how students demonstrate their learning (Tomlinson, 1999).

When we differentiate instruction, we create multiple pathways to learning. Doing this supports our goal of helping students to perform to their maximum potentials.

Variety of Texts at a Diversity of Levels   Students benefit from engaging daily with multiple types and levels of text. Experience in reading texts from multiple genres provides students with knowledge of various text structures and improves their text-driven processing (Goldman & Rakestraw, 2000). Transacting with a wide variety of genres—including biography, historical fiction, legends, poetry, articles, and brochures—enhances students' motivation and increases their comprehension (Gambrell, 2001). When a leveled text is being used, teachers scaffold learning experiences and students receive varying levels of support, depending on the purpose and instructional setting.

We provide independent-level or easy texts when students are working on their own in literacy centers or routines. Students can read texts at this level with no teacher support. We use instructional-level or "just right" texts when students are engaged in guided reading.

Students can read texts at this level with some assistance from the teacher. We do not encourage students to read frustration-level texts, but we can share these more challenging texts in several ways, including teacher read-alouds, cross-age experiences, small-group close reading, and as books on CD.

It is important to note that student interest plays a role in text selection. To determine individual interests, invite students to complete interest inventories, literacy histories, or interviews. Use the information gleaned from these activities to inform your selections when choosing new books for your classroom library and to make recommendations to the school or community librarian, as well as to parents.

Multiple Representations of Thinking   We often ask our students to provide oral or written responses to the texts they read, because those typically are the most frequently used response modes. Although oral and written responses are fine, we also need to offer students alternative modes of response, including sketching, dramatizing, singing, and designing projects.

Because we do not all learn in the same way, the same instructional environment, methods, and resources are effective for some learners and ineffective for others (Burke & Dunn, 2003). Offering students opportunities to express their thoughts through multiple modes of representation allows them to choose their strength modalities when expressing their ideas. Offering multiple modes of response is motivational for all students, but it is particularly beneficial for struggling readers.

Meaningful Contexts   Duke (2001) has delineated an expanded understanding of context for present-day learners. Specifically, she suggests that context should be viewed as curriculum, activity, classroom environment, teachers and teaching, text, and society. One of the most interesting aspects of this expanded notion of context is the number of influences that impact student learning. As Cambourne (2002) reminds us, "What is learned cannot be separated from the context in which it is learned" (p. 26).

Lipson and Wixson (2009) describe the instructional context as including settings, practices, and resources. *Instructional settings* include teacher beliefs and a literate environment, as well as classroom interaction, organization, and grouping. Instructional goals, methods, activities, and assessment practices are all *instructional practices*. Commercial programs, trade materials, and technology are viewed as *instructional resources*.

More specific literacy-based descriptions of context have been offered by Gambrell (1996), Hiebert (1994), and Pearson (2001a). They suggest that the classroom context is characterized by multiple factors, including the classroom organization and authentic opportunities to read, write, and discuss. Other contextual components include instruction in skills and strategies, integration of concept-driven vocabulary, use of multiple genres, and knowledge of various text structures.

Comprehending at Deeper Levels   Current thinking about reading suggests that we should also teach our students to comprehend at deeper levels—levels that require readers to understand beyond the information on the printed page or screen—and to critically analyze the author's message (Luke & Freebody, 1999; McLaughlin & DeVoogd, 2004, 2011). In *critical literacy,* an approach that promotes deeper comprehension, readers move beyond passively accepting the message of a text to question, examine, or dispute the power relationship that exists between the readers and the author. These readers ponder what the author wants them to believe, act on what they believe, and promote fairness between people. Critical literacy focuses on the problem and its complexity. It addresses issues of power and promotes reflection, action, and transformation (Freire, 1970).

Reading from a critical perspective involves thinking beyond the text to understand such issues as why the author wrote about a particular topic, why he or she wrote from a particular perspective, and why certain ideas about the topic were included and others were not. Becoming critically literate means that readers do not passively accept information imparted by others but rather question the source of the ideas, examine who is represented and who is marginalized, and then take action.

Reading from this perspective requires having both the ability and the deliberate inclination to think critically about to analyze and evaluate the power relationship that exists between the reader and the author. Those who read from a critical stance know that though the author has the power to create and present the message, the reader has the power and the right to be a text critic: to read, question, and analyze the author's message. Understanding this power relationship is the essence of critical literacy.

The teacher plays a multifaceted role in initiating and developing critical literacy. It begins with personal understanding and use of critical literacy, and it extends to teaching students about critical literacy. This involves modeling reading from a critical stance in everyday teaching and learning experiences, and providing students with access to a variety of texts that represent critical literacy. When examining the teacher's role, it is important to note that we cannot just "become critical." Developing critical literacy is a process that involves learning, understanding, and changing over time. This includes developing theoretical, research, and pedagogical repertoires; changing with time and circumstance; engaging in self-criticism and self-analysis; and remaining open to possibilities (Comber, 2001).

Once the teacher has become critically aware, teaching students to read from a critical stance should be a natural process. First, as with any other act of reading, the teacher should ensure that students have the background knowledge necessary to comprehend text from a critical stance. The teacher might then choose to scaffold learning by using a five-step instructional framework, as noted earlier: explain, demonstrate, guide, practice, and reflect (McLaughlin & Allen, 2009). Gradually releasing responsibility to the students provides the time and opportunity for them to become comfortable with reading from a critical stance. To begin, the teacher explains what it means to be critically aware and then demonstrate this awareness by using a read-aloud and a think-aloud. During this process, the teacher provides a critical perspective that questions and challenges the text, asking questions such as the following:

- Whose viewpoint is expressed?
- Whose voices are missing, silenced, or discounted?
- What action might you take based on what you have learned?

After the teacher explains and demonstrates, students work in pairs or small groups and offer responses to the questions. The teacher continues to guide their reading as they practice reading from a critical stance. As a final step, the teacher and students reflect on what they know about being critically aware and how it help them to understand the text at deeper levels. This often leads to discussions of how they can apply what they have learned to reading other texts.

Students who engage in critical literacy become open-minded, active, strategic readers who are capable of comprehending text at deeper levels. They understand that the information presented in texts—including not only books but also magazines, newspapers, song lyrics, and websites—has been written from a particular perspective for a particular purpose. They know that meaning is "grounded in the social, political, cultural, and historic contexts of the reading event" (Serafini, 2003, n.p.). The goal is for readers to become text critics in everyday life—to naturally comprehend information sources from a critical stance. As David Pearson (2001a) suggests, comprehension is not enough. It must have a critical edge.

Creating Rich Instructional Tasks

THE COMMON CORE STATE STANDARDS ARE BASED ON an integrated model of language arts. So, it is logical that CCSS-based reading lessons for grades 6–8 should be designed as rich instructional tasks that address multiple standards. For example, a life science lesson might integrate the CCSS identified in Table 2.4. A wide range of reading comprehension strategies can be included in such rich instructional tasks. The following sections describe specific strategies and provide examples of their use in the classroom.

Bookmark Technique   Monitoring is a reading comprehension strategy students use to ensure they are making sense while reading text. Bookmark Technique (McLaughlin & Allen, 2009) is a strategy application in which students monitor their understanding and evaluate specific aspects of text. Typically employed during and after reading informational text, this strategy application provides support to guide students' thinking as they are reading.

TABLE 2.4 ● *Examples of Integrating the Common Core State Standards for Grades 6–8 in a Rich Instructional Task in Science*

- **Reading Informational Text Standard 1:** Cite textual evidence to support analysis of a text.
- **Reading Informational Text Standard 2:** Determine central ideas in a text and analyze their development; provide an objective summary of a text.
- **Writing Standard 2:** Write a clearly developed and well-organized informative/explanatory text.
- **Speaking and Listening Standard 1:** Engage in a variety of types of collaborative discussions.
- **Speaking and Listening Standard 5:** Include multiple types of media and visual displays in presentations.
- **Language Standard 4:** Determine or clarify the meanings of unknown and multiple-meaning words and phrases.
- **Language Standard 6:** Learn and use grade-appropriate academic and domain-specific words and phrases.

In Bookmark Technique, students create four bookmarks:

- On Bookmark 1, students record what they found most interesting about the text.
- On Bookmark 2, the students choose a vocabulary word that they think everyone in the class needs to discuss.
- On Bookmark 3, the students record an illustration, chart, map, or graph that helped them to understand what they read.
- On Bookmark 4, the students note something in the text that they found confusing.

Students also record the page and paragraph where the information appears on each Bookmark. As an alternative mode of response, students can also sketch their responses on their bookmarks. Figure 2.1 shows four bookmarks completed in response to reading about a topic in American history.

When students complete their bookmarks, they all have four pieces of information to share in whole-class or small-group discussion, which contributes to the social construction of meaning. The completed Bookmarks also provide evidence that students have read the text. Students are motivated by the opportunities that Bookmark Technique offers to express their individual thoughts and make personal choices about the text they are reading.

Lyric Summary   Summarizing is a vital reading comprehension strategy. The Lyric Summary is a strategy application that provides students with the opportunity to create

FIGURE 2.1 • Example of the Bookmark Technique Using a Text in American History

Text: *American History of Our Nation: Beginnings through 1877* (Davidson, 2009)

Bookmark 1

> **Bookmark 1**
>
> The most interesting part was . . .
>
> *I think that when George Washington took office as the first President of the United States and set up the three departments of the executive branch: Treasury, State, and War is the most interesting part, because that action became the foundation of our government.*
>
> **Page** 283
> **Paragraph** 3

Bookmark 2

> **Bookmark 2**
>
> A vocabulary word I think the whole class needs to discuss is . . .
>
> *I think the class should discuss invested. I know that it means to buy something and hope that it will increase in value. People invested in government bonds and hoped that their value would grow.*
>
> **Page** 284
> **Paragraph** 2

Bookmark 3

> **Bookmark 3**
>
> The illustration, chart, map, or graph that helped me understand what I was reading was . . .
>
> *I think the chart that showed me the amount of money it cost to run the government, the amount of money that the United States owed, and the income that the United States received helped me to understand that the United States needed more income to pay back its debt.*
>
> **Page** 284
> **Paragraph** 4

Bookmark 4

> **Bookmark 4**
>
> Something that confused me was . . .
>
> *It confused me when the book stated that people had sold their bonds for less than they had originally paid, because the book stated that the government promised to pay back all of the money for the bonds with interest.*
>
> **Page** 284
> **Paragraph** 2

FIGURE 2.2 ● Lyric Summary about Bacteria

Text: *Biology* (Miller & Levine, 2008)

Song: "The Facts of Life," by Alan Thicke, Gloria Loring, and Al Burton; sung by Gloria Loring (available online at http://classic-tv.com)

You can have bacteria, it's not all bad,

There are two types and there you have

microscopic life, microscopic life.

Prokaryotes the smallest form is now

divided in two groups, let's shout

microscopic life, microscopic life.

When eubacteria is the largest, it seems

and achaebacteria is chemically different it's foreseen

that suddenly we're finding out

bacteria's vital to maintain the world, world.

Producers of energy, that's right

decomposers, nitrogen fixers, and human uses for life

Learning about microscopic life

Learning about microscopic life.

an objective summary (McLaughlin & Allen, 2009). In this strategy application, students gather in small groups after learning about a particular topic. To begin, students work in small groups and brainstorm individual lists of information about the topic. Next, they choose a song—a melody that everyone in the group knows. Then, they use their brainstormed lists to write new lyrics for the song.

Of course, the only way to share Lyric Summaries is to sing them, so each group does exactly that. Figure 2.2 shows a Lyric Summary that students created about the topic *bacteria*.

Venn Diagram   The Venn Diagram is a graphic organizer that illustrates the similarities and differences of two topics. The similarities are written in the overlapping part of the circles (comparison), and the differences are recorded in the outer portions of each circle (contrast). Figure 2.3 shows a Venn diagram about the topic *rocks*.

FIGURE 2.3 ● Venn Diagram about Rocks

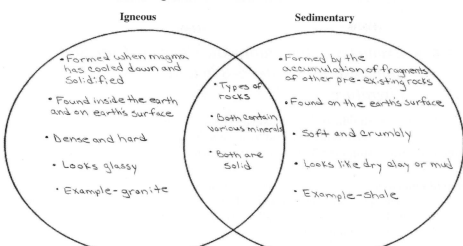

Igneous   Sedimentary

- Formed when magma has cooled down and solidified
- Found inside the earth and on earth's surface
- Dense and hard
- Looks glassy
- Example- granite

- Types of rocks
- Both contain various minerals
- Both are solid

- Formed by the accumulation of fragments of other pre-existing rocks
- Found on the earth's surface
- Soft and crumbly
- Looks like dry clay or mud
- Example- Shale

The Venn Diagram can also be used as the basis of an oral or written summary. This graphic organizer is also an appropriate representation of the *comparison/contrast* informational text structure, knowledge of which is an expectation of the Common Core.

To create rich instructional tasks in literature, we might integrate the Common Core State Standards identified in Table 2.5. During a lesson based on these standards, we could invite students to do the following:

- Quote from the text to support analysis of what the text says explicitly.
- Analyze how the setting (including the place and time) shapes the characters.
- Write a sequel or "next episode" for the story that includes descriptive details.
- Use the writing process when creating the sequel or "next episode."
- Engage in different types of collaborative discussions throughout the lesson. Share a sequel or "next episode" in a PowerPoint slide show that integrates multiple media that relate to and support the writing.
- Determine or clarify selected vocabulary featured in the original story.

Making Connections   Making Connections is a reading comprehension strategy that students use to activate background knowledge and link it to the information they are reading. Sketching Connections (McLaughlin & Allen, 2009) is a strategy application that can be used as an alternative mode of representing ideas found in a text. Figure 2.4 features an example of Sketching Connections based on the book *Roll of Thunder, Hear My Cry* (Taylor, 2004). Using sketching as an alternative mode of representation motivates students to respond.

TABLE 2.5 ● *Examples of Integrating the Common Core State Standards for Grades 6–8 in a Rich Instructional Task in Literature*

- **Reading Literature Standard 1:** Cite textual evidence to support analysis of what the text says explicitly as well as inferences drawn from the text.
- **Reading Literature Standard 3:** Analyze how particular elements of a story or drama interact.
- **Writing Standard 3:** Write narratives to develop real or imagined experiences or events, using effective techniques, relevant descriptive details, and well-structured event sequences.
- **Writing Standard 5:** Develop and strengthen writing by planning, revising, editing, rewriting, or trying a new approach, focusing on how well purpose and audience have been addressed.
- **Speaking and Listening Standard 1:** Engage in a variety of collaborative discussions.
- **Speaking and Listening Standard 5:** Include multiple types of media and visual displays in presentations.
- **Language Standard 4:** Determine or clarify the meanings of unknown and multiple-meaning words and phrases.

FIGURE 2.4 ● Sketching Connections in *Roll of Thunder, Hear My Cry*

I drew a picture of a tree after reading Chapter 9, because to me it represents how trees can be very different and grow beautifully next to each other like people do. Cassie's father also explains to her that every tree/person deserves to grow and live and should never give up because of its size/differences. The tree also represents roots and how important it was for Cassie's family to own their own land.

In the Common Core Classroom

Sean is a sixth-grade, middle school science teacher who has worked extensively with colleagues to implement the Common Core. As he began to include the CCSS in his planning, he realized that this was the first time his students would be expected to meet the Common Core. Given this, Sean was particularly careful to read the Standards horizontally. He wanted to ensure that his students could meet all of the expectations of the CCSS for sixth-grade students, including those designed for grades K–5.

When designing the rich instructional task that included the following lesson and related class project, Sean integrated Common Core State Reading Standard 1 for both Literature and Informational Text for grades K–3, which addresses asking and answering questions about a text. He also integrated the following CCSS for grade 6 in the lesson and project:

- Reading Informational Text: Standards 1, 4 (lesson and project)
- Writing: Standards 2a–f, 4, 5, 6 (lesson: Standard 4; project: all Standards)
- Speaking and Listening: Standards 1a–d, 5 (lesson and project: Standard 1; project: Standard 5)
- Language: Standards 1, 3, 4, 6 (lesson and project)

As Sean and his colleagues worked together to learn about the Common Core State Standards, they read the standards vertically to understand the expectations for students at their grade level and horizontally to understand what the standards assumed their students would know. The teachers became concerned that their students were not adept at generating and responding to questions at multiple levels. After engaging in an in-depth discussion with his students, Sean realized that although they knew how to ask and answer questions at the literal level, they did not know how to employ that skill using higher levels of thinking. (Asking and answering questions is the focus of Reading Standard 1 for grades K–3, although applying multiple levels of thinking is not mentioned.)

Sean began by discussing questioning with his students. It was early in the school year, but the students would soon be engaging in research projects in science. Each student would choose a female scientist, research her contributions to the field, and report these findings in a PowerPoint slide show or other medium of his or her choosing. Sean decided to situate his teaching of questioning within the research project.

To engage students and help them to activate their background knowledge, Sean asked them to work with partners to brainstorm questions they could use to guide their research. Students readily shared their ideas. Questions included when the scientist was born, when she died, and what scientific contribution she was known for. Sean knew immediately that he needed to teach his students how to generate and respond to questions using multiple levels of thinking. He used this information to create a series of lessons to teach his students about generating and responding to questions at multiple levels. He framed his teaching using the five-step model for explicit strategy instruction (McLaughlin & Allen, 2009).

Providing explicit instruction, Sean taught his students how to create questions at the convergent level. He used his students' literal-level questions to launch asking question at the next level. He explained convergent questions as those that begin with *why* and *how.* He also noted that questions at this level can be used to compare and contrast information.

Next, Sean demonstrated by using Albert Einstein's biography, appropriate signal words, and a think-aloud (Davey, 1983) to model how to create convergent levels questions. (One useful online source of biographies is the website Biography.com [www.biography.com].) Here are some examples of convergent questions that Sean generated:

- Why was Albert Einstein considered a school dropout?
- How did this affect his enrolling at his next school?

After discussing these questions with his students, Sean guided them to work with partners to create two convergent questions about another section of the Einstein text, offering support as needed. He encouraged students to use the signal words to begin their questions. After the students had generated their own questions, they shared what they had created. Here are several of the students' questions:

- Why did Einstein begin thinking about relativity?
- Why was 1905 called Einstein's "miracle year?"
- How was Einstein successful in becoming respected in the academic world?

Sean noted, "It was as if light bulbs were turning on all over the room! The students clearly understood how to structure the questions." Next, Sean shared an additional section of the text and encouraged students to practice by creating convergent-level questions on their own.

Sean followed up by teaching his students about Thick and Thin Questions (Lewin, 1998). Thin questions would, as always, be literal-level, memory questions. At this point in students' learning, the thick questions would be limited to convergent-level questions. Sean provided an electronic biography for students' use in this part of the lesson. When students felt comfortable generating and responding to convergent questions, Sean moved on to teaching about divergent and evaluative questions. Students wrote several of these types of questions, including the following:

- **Divergent level:** Imagine that Einstein did not make the scientific discoveries for which he is known. How would our world be different?

- **Evaluative level:** Einstein said: "The world is a dangerous place to live; not because of the people who are evil, but because of the people who don't do anything about it." Do you agree or disagree? Justify your position.

  The class also discussed chronology as a text structure (Reading Informational Text Standard 5 for grades 4–5) to assist students with their research projects. Sean recognized that grade 5 is the last grade for which the CCSS include text structures. "So, technically," he stated, "knowing text structures is not a grade 6–8 skill, but in real life, students in grades 6–12 do need to know and be able to use text structures. This is an example of a gap in the Standards."

  As Sean taught the levels of questioning and chronology as a text structure, it became clear that he should discuss these topics each year before the start of students' science research projects. That way, he would be able to assess what his students already know about these topics and then decide whether he needed to teach them.

Comprehending text is an essential skill for students in grades 6–8. The authors of the CCSS note that the teaching of reading comprehension is not included in the Standards but rather is left in teachers' hands. We need to embrace this responsibility to ensure that our students are college and career ready.

REFERENCES

Anderson, R. C. (2004). Role of reader's schema in comprehension, learning, and memory. In R. B. Ruddell, M. R. Ruddell, & H. Singer (Eds.), *Theoretical models and processes of reading* (5th ed., pp. 594–606). Newark, DE: International Reading Association.

Anderson, R. C., & Pearson, P. D. (1984). A schema-theoretic view of basic processes in reading comprehension. In P. D. Pearson, R. Barr, M. L. Kamil, & P. Mosenthal (Eds.), *Handbook of reading research* (pp. 225–253). New York, NY: Longman.

Au, K. H., & Raphael, T. E. (1998). Curriculum and teaching in literature-based programs. In T. E. Raphael & K. H. Au (Eds.), *Literature-based instruction: Reshaping the curriculum* (pp. 123–148). Norwood, MA: Christopher-Gordon.

Baker, L., Afflerbach, P., & Reinking, D. (1996). Developing engaged readers in school and home communities: An overview. In L. Baker, P. Afflerbach, & D. Reinking (Eds.), *Developing engaged readers in school and home communities* (pp. xiii–xxvii). Hillsdale, NJ: Erlbaum.

Baker, L., & Wigfield, A. (1999). Dimensions of children's motivation for reading and their relations to reading activity and reading achievement. *Reading Research Quarterly, 34,* 452–481.

Biancarosa, C., & Snow, C. E. (2006). *Reading next—A vision for action and research in middle and high school literacy: A report to Carnegie Corporation of New York* (2nd ed.). Washington, DC: Alliance for Excellent Education.

Burke, K., & Dunn, R. (2003). Learning style-based teaching to raise minority student test scores. *The Social Studies, 94,* 167–170.

Cambourne, B. (2002). Holistic, integrated approaches to reading and language arts instruction: The constructivist framework of an instructional theory. In A. E. Farstrup & S. J. Samuels (Eds.), *What research has to say about reading instruction* (3rd ed., pp. 25–47). Newark, DE: International Reading Association.

Comber, B. (2001). Critical literacies and local action: Teacher knowledge and a "new" research agenda. In B. Comber & A. Simpson (Eds.), *Negotiating critical literacies in classrooms* (pp. 271–282). Mahwah, NJ: Erlbaum.

Dahl, K. L., & Farnan, N. (1998). *Children's writing: Perspectives from research.* Newark, DE: International Reading Association.

Davey, B. (1983). Think-aloud—Demonstrating the cognitive processes of reading comprehension. *Journal of Reading, 27,* 44–47.

Duke, N. (2001, December). *A new generation of researchers looks at comprehension.* Paper presented at the annual meeting of the National Reading Conference, San Antonio, TX.

Duke, N. K., & Pearson, P. D. (2002). Effective practices for developing reading comprehension. In A. E. Farstrup & S. J. Samuels (Eds.), *What research has to say about reading instruction* (3rd ed., pp. 205–242). Newark, DE: International Reading Association.

Duke, N., Pressley, M., & Hilden, K. (2004). Difficulties with reading comprehension. In C. A. Stone, E. R. Silliman, B. J. Ehren, & K. Apel (Eds.), *Handbook of language and literacy: Development and disorders* (pp. 501–520). New York, NY: Guilford.

Durkin, D. (1978/1979). What classroom observations reveal about reading comprehension instruction. *Reading Research Quarterly, 14,* 481–533.

Freire, P. (1970). *Pedagogy of the oppressed.* New York, NY: Continuum.

Gambrell, L. B. (1996). Creating classroom cultures that foster reading motivation. *The Reading Teacher, 50*(1), 14–25.

Gambrell, L. B. (2001). *It's not either/or but more: Balancing narrative and informational text to improve reading comprehension.* Paper presented at the annual convention of the International Reading Association, New Orleans, LA.

Gambrell, L. B. (2011a). Motivation in the school reading curriculum. In T. V. Rasinski (Ed.), *Rebuilding the foundation: Effective reading instruction for 21st century literacy* (pp. 41–65). Bloomington, IN: Solution Tree Press.

Gambrell, L. B. (2011b). Seven rules of engagement: What's most important to know about motivation to read. *The Reading Teacher, 65*(3), 172–178.

Gambrell, L. B., Palmer, B. M., Codling, R. M., & Mazzoni, S. A. (1996). Assessing motivation to read. *The Reading Teacher, 49*(7), 518–533.

Gibson, V., & Hasbrouck, J. (2008). *Differentiated instruction: Grouping for success.* New York, NY: McGraw-Hill.

Goldman, S. R., & Rakestraw, J. A. (2000). Structural aspects of constructing meaning from text. In M. L. Kamil, P. D. Pearson, & R. Barr (Eds.), *Handbook of reading research: Vol. 3* (pp. 311–335). Mahwah, NJ: Erlbaum.

Guthrie, J. T., & Alvermann, D. (Eds.). (1999). *Engagement in reading: Processes, practices, and policy implications.* New York, NY: Teachers College Press.

Guthrie, J. T., & Humenick, N. M. (2004). Motivating students to read: Evidence for classroom practices that increase motivation. In P. McCardle & V. Chhabra (Eds.), *The voice of evidence in reading research* (pp. 329–354). Baltimore, MD: Brookes.

Guthrie, J. T., & Wigfield, A. (Eds.). (1997). *Reading engagement: Motivating readers through integrated instruction.* Newark, DE: International Reading Association.

Harris, T. L., & Hodges, R. E. (Eds.). (1995). *The literacy dictionary: The vocabulary of reading and writing.* Newark, DE: International Reading Association.

Hiebert, E. H. (1994). Becoming literate through authentic tasks: Evidence and adaptations. In R. B. Ruddell, M. R. Ruddell, & H. Singer (Eds.), *Theoretical models and processes of reading* (pp. 391–413). Newark, DE: International Reading Association.

Hilden, K., & Pressley, M. (2002, December). *Can teachers become comprehension strategies teachers given a small amount of training?* Paper presented at the annual meeting of the National Reading Conference, Miami, FL.

International Reading Association. (2000). *Excellent reading teachers: A position statement of the International Reading Association.* Newark, DE: Author.

Lewin, L. (1998). *Great performances: Creating classroom-based assessment tasks.* Alexandria, VA: Association for Supervision and Curriculum Development.

Lipson, M. Y., & Wixson, K. K. (2009). *Assessment and instruction of reading and writing difficulties: An interactive approach* (4th ed.). Boston, MA: Allyn & Bacon.

Luke, A., & Freebody, P. (1999, August). Further notes on the four resources model. *Reading Online.* Retrieved from www.readingonline.org/research/lukefreebody.html.

McKeown, M. G., Beck, I. L., & Blake, R. G. K. (2009). Rethinking reading comprehension instruction: A comparison of instruction for strategies and content approaches. *Reading Research Quarterly, 44*(3), 218–253.

McLaughlin, M. (2003). *Guided Comprehension in the primary grades: A framework for curricularizing strategy instruction.* Paper presented at the annual meeting of the National Reading Conference, Scottsdale, AZ.

McLaughlin, M. (2010a). *Content area reading: Teaching and learning in an age of multiple literacies.* Boston, MA: Allyn & Bacon.

McLaughlin, M. (2010b). *Guided Comprehension in the primary grades* (2nd ed.). Newark, DE: International Reading Association.

McLaughlin, M. (2012). Reading comprehension: What every teacher needs to know. *The Reading Teacher, 65*(7), 432–440.

McLaughlin, M., & Allen, M. B. (2009). *Guided Comprehension in grades 3–8* (2nd ed.). Newark, DE: International Reading Association.

McLaughlin, M., & DeVoogd, G. (2004). *Critical literacy: Enhancing students' reading comprehension.* New York, NY: Scholastic.

McLaughlin, M., & DeVoogd, G. (2011). Critical literacy as comprehension: Understanding at deeper levels. In D. Lapp & D. Fisher (Eds.), *The handbook of research on teaching the English language arts* (3rd ed., pp. 278–282). New York, NY: Routledge.

National Governors Association Center for Best Practices & Council of Chief State School Officers (NGA & CCSSO). (2010). *Common Core State Standards: English language arts and literacy in history/social studies, science, and technical subjects.* Washington, DC: Authors. Retrieved from www.corestandards.org/assets/CCSSI_ELA%20Standards.pdf.

Palincsar, A. S., & Brown, A. L. (1984). Reciprocal teaching of comprehension fostering and monitoring activities. *Cognition and Instruction, 1,* 117–175.

Paris, A., & Paris, S. (2007). Teaching narrative comprehension strategies to first graders. *Cognition and Instruction, 25*(1), 1–44.

Pearson, P. D. (2001a, December). *What we have learned in 30 years.* Paper presented at the annual meeting of the National Reading Conference, San Antonio, TX.

Pearson, P. D. (2001b, February). *Comprehension strategy instruction: An idea whose time has come again.* Paper presented at the annual meeting of the Colorado Council of the International Reading Association, Denver, CO.

Pearson, P. D., & Hoffman, J. V. (2011). Principles of practice for the teaching of reading. In T.V. Rasinski (Ed.). *Rebuilding the foundation: Effective reading instruction for 21st century literacy* (pp. 9–38). Bloomington, IN: Solution Tree Press.

Pressley, M. (2000). What should comprehension instruction be the instruction of? In M. L. Kamil, P. B. Mosenthal, P. D. Pearson, & R. Barr (Eds.), *Handbook of reading research: Vol. 3* (pp. 545–561). Mahwah, NJ: Erlbaum.

Pressley, M. (2006, April). *What the future of reading research could be.* Paper presented at the International Reading Association Reading Research Conference, Chicago, IL.

Roehler, L. R., & Duffy, G. G. (1984). Direct explanation of comprehension processes. In G. G. Duffy, L. R. Roehler, & J. Mason (Eds.), *Comprehension instruction: Perspectives and suggestions* (pp. 265–280). New York, NY: Longman.

Ruddell, R. B. (1995). Those influential literacy teachers: Meaning negotiators and motivation builders. *The Reading Teacher, 48,* 454–463.

Ruddell, R. B. (2004). Researching the influential literacy teacher: Characteristics, beliefs, strategies, and new research directions. In R. B. Ruddell & N. J. Unrau (Eds.), *Theoretical models and processes of reading* (5th ed., pp. 979–997). Newark, DE: International Reading Association.

Serafini, F. (2003, February). Informing our practice: Modernist, transactional, and critical perspectives on children's literature and reading instruction. *Reading Online, 6*(6). Retrieved from http://www.readingonline.org/articles/art_index.asp?HREF=serafini/index.html.

Tomlinson, C. A. (1999). *The differentiated classroom: Responding to the needs of all learners.* Alexandria, VA: Association for Supervision and Curriculum Development.

Tyner, B., & Green, S. E. (2009). *Small-group reading instruction: A differentiated model for intermediate readers, grades 3–8* (2nd ed.). Newark, DE: International Reading Association.

Vygotsky, L. S. (1978). *Mind in society: The development of higher psychological processes* (M. Cole, V. John-Steiner, S. Scribner, & E. Souberman, Eds.). Cambridge, MA: Harvard University Press. (Original work published 1934)

LITERATURE AND INFORMATIONAL TEXTS CITED

Albert Einstein. (2012). *Biography.com.* Retrieved from http://www.biography.com/people/ albert-einstein-9285408.

Davidson, J. W. (2009). *American history of our nation: Beginnings through 1877.* Boston, MA: Prentice-Hall.

Miller, K. R., & Levine, J. S. (2008). *Biology.* Boston, MA: Prentice-Hall.

Taylor, M. (2004). *Roll of thunder, hear my cry.* New York, NY: Puffin.

chapter 3

Vocabulary

WHEN WE THINK ABOUT VOCABULARY IN RELATION to the Common Core State Standards (CCSS), we should begin by acknowledging that this subject is addressed in three different strands of the Standards: Language, Reading, and Writing. We should also note that although the CCSS do address vocabulary, they do not cover everything our students need to know about vocabulary. As noted in Chapter 1, the writers of the CCSS created the standards, but they left the teaching in our hands—including the teaching of vocabulary.

Our goal in this chapter is to situate the Common Core State Standards within the research, theory, and practice involved in teaching vocabulary. To achieve this, we will examine what students need to know about vocabulary to successfully meet the expectations of the Common Core.

Monkey Business/Fotolia

This chapter is divided into four sections. In the first section, we outline what the CCSS have to say about vocabulary. Next, we examine what we know about teaching vocabulary. Then we explore teaching ideas and classroom examples that support vocabulary, as it is addressed in the Common Core. Finally, we consider *Inside the Common Core Classroom,* a vignette that illustrates one classroom teacher's choices for teaching to the Common Core.

The Common Core and Vocabulary

VOCABULARY IS UNIQUELY REPRESENTED IN THE CCSS, because it is a focus in three different strands: Language, Reading, and Writing (NGA & CCSSO, 2010). Discussions follow of the CCSS for grade 8 that address vocabulary.

Language Standards

In the CCSS Language Standards, vocabulary is addressed in the cluster or category Vocabulary Acquisition and Use, which includes standards 4, 5, and 6 (see Table 3.1) (NGA & CCSSO, 2010). As stated in Standard 4, students in grade 8 are expected to have multiple skills in determining word meanings. To begin, students are expected to be able to use context clues to determine the meanings of words. They are also expected to use generative word parts (e.g., prefixes, roots, and suffixes) to determine the meanings of words. Students should also be able to use reference books (e.g., dictionaries and thesauruses) to find pronunciations and clarify meanings of words. Finally, students are expected to determine preliminary word meanings using context clues or a dictionary.

In Language Standard 5, students in grade 8 are expected to understand figurative language, word relationships, and nuances in word meanings. This includes interpreting figures of speech in context and determining differences between denotations and connotations.

Students are expected to learn and be able to use grade appropriate academic and domain-specific vocabulary in Language Standard 6. This includes particular emphasis on knowledge of vocabulary related to comprehension and expression.

Reading Standards

In the CCSS Reading standards, vocabulary is addressed in both the Literature and the Informational Text substrands in Standard 4, which is within the cluster Craft and Structure (see Table 3.2) (NGA & CCSSO, 2010). According to these vocabulary-related standards, students are expected to determine the meanings of words as they appear in text. Once again, doing so involves the use of context clues, but this time, the skill is extended to include figurative, connotative, and technical meanings. Students are also expected to analyze the effect of the author's word choices on meaning and tone in both narrative and informational texts; this includes analogies and allusions to other texts.

TABLE 3.1 ● *Common Core State Standards for Language:* Vocabulary Acquisition and Use, Grade 8

Grade 8 Students:

Vocabulary Acquisition and Use

4. Determine or clarify the meaning of unknown and multiple-meaning words or phrases based on grade 8 reading and content, choosing flexibly from a range of strategies.

   a. Use context (e.g., the overall meaning of a sentence or paragraph; a word's position or function in a sentence) as a clue to the meaning of a word or phrase.

   b. Use common, grade-appropriate Greek or Latin affixes and roots as clues to the meaning of a word (e.g., *precede, recede, secede*).

   c. Consult general and specialized reference materials (e.g., dictionaries, glossaries, thesauruses), both print and digital, to find the pronunciation of a word or determine or clarify its precise meaning or its part of speech.

   d. Verify the preliminary determination of the meaning of a word or phrase (e.g., by checking the inferred meaning in context or in a dictionary).

5. Demonstrate understanding of figurative language, word relationships, and nuances in word meanings.

   a. Interpret figures of speech (e.g. verbal irony, puns) in context.

   b. Use the relationship between particular words to better understand each of the words.

   c. Distinguish among the connotations (associations) of words with similar denotations (definitions) (e.g., *bullheaded, willful, firm, persistent, resolute*).

6. Acquire and use accurately grade-appropriate general academic and domain-specific words and phrases; gather vocabulary knowledge when considering a word or phrase important to comprehension or expression.

TABLE 3.2 ● *Vocabulary-Related Common Core State Standards for Reading, Grade 8*

Grade 8 Students:

Reading Literature: Craft and Structure

4. Determine the meaning of words and phrases as they are used in a text, including figurative and connotative meanings; analyze the impact of specific word choices on meaning and tone, including analogies or allusions to other texts.

Reading Informational Text: Craft and Structure

4. Determine the meaning of words and phrases as they are used in a text, including figurative, connotative, and technical meanings; analyze the impact of specific word choices on meaning and tone, including analogies or allusions to other texts.

TABLE 3.3 ● *Vocabulary-Related Common Core State Standards for Writing, Grade 8*

Grade 8 Students:
Text Types and Purposes

2. Write informative/explanatory texts to examine a topic and convey ideas, concepts, and information through the selection, organization, and analysis of relevant content.

    d. Use precise language and domain-specific vocabulary to inform about or explain the topic.

Writing Standard

The CCSS Writing standard that addresses vocabulary is Standard 2d, which is within the cluster Text Types and Purposes (see Table 3.3) (NGA & CCSSO, 2010). According to this standard, students should be able to use what they know about vocabulary when writing informational text for a variety of purposes. Students are also responsible for using precise language and domain-specific vocabulary when writing to inform or explain.

What We Know about the Teaching of Vocabulary

RESEARCHERS AGREE THAT IF STUDENTS DO NOT KNOW THE WORDS in a given context, they will have difficulty comprehending what they are reading (Dixon-Krauss, 2001/2002; Duke, 2007; McLaughlin & Allen, 2009; Richek, 2005). Vocabulary instruction leads to gains in comprehension, but the methods must be appropriate to the age and ability of the reader (NICHD, 2000).

A number of researchers have concluded that reading widely is an effective way to promote vocabulary growth (Blachowicz, Fisher, Ogle, & Watts-Taffe, 2006; Kucan, 2012). Consequently, one of our continuing goals when teaching vocabulary is to ensure that students read a wide range of materials on a frequent basis. We should also continue to engage in teacher read-alouds to share ideas, stimulate discussion, and introduce students to new words in context.

Vocabulary development and instruction have strong ties to reading comprehension. As the National Reading Panel (NICHD, 2000) reports, "Reading comprehension is a complex, cognitive process that cannot be understood without a clear description of the role that vocabulary development and vocabulary instruction play in the understanding of what has been read" (p. 13). Snow, Burns, and Griffin (1998) support this view; in their words, "Learning new concepts and words that encode them is essential to comprehension development" (p. 217).

Pearson, Hiebert, and Kamil (2007) note that vocabulary may seem simple but is actually complex. Words relate to our experiences and knowledge, and their meanings change depending on the contexts in which they are used. These authors further note that there are four types of vocabulary: listening, speaking, reading, and writing. Speaking and writing vocabularies are viewed as productive, and listening and reading as receptive. We typically understand more words through listening and reading than we use in speech and writing. Graves (2006) suggests that "one way to build students' vocabulary is to immerse them in a rich array of language experiences so that they learn words through listening, speaking, reading, and writing" (p. 5).

Vocabulary Development and Word Consciousness

As described by Harris and Hodges (1995), vocabulary development involves two elements: "(1) the growth of a person's stock of known words and meanings; (2) the teaching-learning principles and practices that lead to such growth, as comparing and classifying word meanings, using context, analyzing root words and affixes, etc." (p. 275). Blachowicz et al. (2006) also share several facts about the development of vocabulary knowledge that are well grounded in research:

- Knowledge of vocabulary is a significant predictor of students' comprehension.
- The gap in vocabulary knowledge between economic groups correlates with poor school performance.
- Vocabulary knowledge is essential for the academic success of English learners. Depending on the nature of the text, vocabulary knowledge differentially impacts students' reading comprehension in school.

Vocabulary development is influenced by the amount and variety of texts that students read (Baumann & Kame'enui, 1991; Beck & McKeown, 1991; Beck, McLeown, & Kucan, 2002, 2008; Snow et al., 1998). Teacher read-alouds, which offer students access to a variety of levels of texts, also contribute to the process of vocabulary development (Hiebert, Pearson, Taylor, Richardson, & Paris, 1998).

Word Consciousness

Word consciousness involves several levels of awareness: an awareness of words and their meanings, an awareness of the ways in which meanings change and grow, and an interest in and motivation to develop new word knowledge. All of these factors support both incidental and intentional word learning (Graves, 2006).

The importance of word consciousness in vocabulary development has been noted by Graves and Watts-Taffe (2002), who also reported that word consciousness involves both cognitive and affective stances toward words. Students who are word conscious are interested in words. They know and use many words, and they also enjoy using words and seeing and hearing words used well by others. Research has confirmed that environments in which language and word use are encouraged and celebrated are also characterized by word consciousness (Graves, 2006; Graves &Watts-Taffe, 2002).

Nurturing word consciousness in our classrooms means making a commitment to developing students' curiosity about words and to discovering what words mean and how they function (Kucan, 2012). Specific strategies for developing word consciousness include the following:

- Modeling, recognizing, and encouraging adept diction
- Promoting word play to reinforce that printed words have meaning
- Providing intensive and expressive instruction (Integrating reading and writing)
- Encouraging students to engage in vocabulary learning as inquiry
- Teaching students about words so they can learn them, manipulate them, appreciate them, and play with them (Graves & Watts-Taffe, 2002, pp. 145- 159)

Effective Vocabulary Instruction

To integrate what we know about vocabulary into our teaching, we should begin by putting research into practice. Blachowicz and Fisher (2000) found that the following four guidelines have emerged from existing research about vocabulary instruction:

1. Encourage students to be active in learning vocabulary and developing their own word knowledge.
2. Engage students in personalizing their learning of vocabulary words.
3. Immerse students in words.
4. Teach students to use multiple sources to learn new words and to build their vocabularies through repeated exposures.

Graves and Watts-Taffe (2002) suggest that effective programs for teaching vocabulary include these four elements:

1. wide reading
2. teaching individual words
3. teaching word-learning strategies
4. fostering word consciousness

Baumann and Kame'enui (1991) recommend that explicit instruction in vocabulary and learning new words from context should be balanced, and Blachowicz and Lee (1991) recommend that instruction should be meaningful to students, include words from students' reading, and focus on a variety of strategies for determining the meanings of unfamiliar words. Another important aspect of effective instruction is making connections between vocabulary words and students' background knowledge.

Blachowicz et al. (2006) suggest that effective vocabulary instruction is characterized by these qualities:

- a learning environment that fosters word consciousness
- students' active participation in the process of learning vocabulary
- an integrated approach in which vocabulary is woven into word learning across the disciplines
- instruction that provides both definitional and contextual information
- teachers who provide multiple exposures to words and numerous, ongoing opportunities to use words

Blachowicz et al. (2006) further suggest that vocabulary programs should be comprehensive, integrated, and schoolwide. A program is considered *integrated* when vocabulary is a core consideration in all subjects and in all grades. A program is considered *comprehensive* when teachers share the same philosophy and engage in similar practices during vocabulary instruction. Finally, a program is considered *schoolwide* when these efforts are supported by the curriculum and the classroom and school organization.

To create a comprehensive, integrated approach to vocabulary instruction, Blachowicz, Fisher, and Watts-Taffe (2011) suggest that teachers engage in these practices:

- Ensure the classroom is full of accountable talk, listening, reading, and writing.
- Intentionally teach individual words.
- Build and strengthen students' word-learning strategies and understanding of the generative word elements, such as roots and affixes.
- Develop word consciousness by introducing categories of word relations.
- Use technology to make word investigations more rewarding. (pp. 215–216)

Kucan (2012) notes that the classrooms of teachers who support students' vocabulary development can be characterized as *"energized verbal environments*—environments in which words are not only noticed and appreciated, but also savored and celebrated" (p. 361).

Word Study

Word study is the active process of examining words; it integrates vocabulary, grammar, and spelling. In addition, it "exercises multiple components of word knowledge, and carries over to reading and writing development" (Bloodgood & Pacifici, 2004, p. 262).

Word study provides insight into how words work. In terms of vocabulary development, understanding which part of speech a word is, how to analyze its structure (i.e., prefixes, roots, suffixes), how to spell it, and what it means helps readers to recognize and understand the word more quickly when they read it in text. Word knowledge should include understanding of roots, affixes (prefixes and suffixes), homonyms (homophones and homographs), and other vocabulary, spelling, and grammatical features. Examples of commonly used prefixes, suffixes, and roots are presented in Tables 3.4, 3.5, and 3.6, respectively.

TABLE 3.4 ● *Commonly Used Prefixes*

Prefix(es)	Meaning(s)	Sample Word
ab-, abs-, a-	from, away	abstain
ad-	to, toward	addict
ambi-	both	ambidextrous
ante-	before	antecedent
anti-	against	antifreeze
auto-	self	autobiography
be-	near, about	beside
bene-	well, good	benefactor
bi-	two	bimonthly
cata-	below	catacomb
centi-	hundred	centimeter
circum-	around	circumnavigate
con-	with	concert
contra-	against	contraband
de-	from, down	depress
deci-	ten	decimeter
di-	two	diameter
dia-	through	diagram
dis-	opposite	disrespect
dys-	bad	dysfunctional
en-, em-	cause to	encode
epi-	upon	epidermis
ex-	out, from	excavate
extra-	beyond	extracurricular
for-	off, to the uttermost	forward
fore-	before	forecast
hetero-	different	heterogeneous
hyper-	beyond, excess	hyperactive
hypo-	too little, under	hypoactive
in-, il-, im-, ir-	not	immature

(continued)

TABLE 3.4 ● *(continued)*

Prefix(es)	Meaning(s)	Sample Word
in-, im-	in	*infringe*
inter-	between	*interstate*
intra-	within	*intramural*
intro-	within	*introspection*
juxta-	near	*juxtapose*
macro-	large	*macrobiology*
meta-	beyond, denoting change	*metamorphosis*
micro-	small	*microbiology*
mid-	middle	*midway*
milli-	thousand	*millipede*
mis-	bad	*misbehave*
mono-	single	*monotone*
nano-	billion	*nanosecond*
neo-	new	*neoclassical*
non-	not, opposite from	*nonviolent*
omni-	all	*omnipotent*
out-	beyond, more than	*outlaw*
over-	too much	*overcompensate*
pan-	all	*panoramic*
para-	side by side, near	*paraphrase*
per-	throughout	*pervade*
peri-	all around	*periscope*
poly-	many	*polygon*
post-	after	*postpone*
pre-	before	*predetermine*
pro-	forward	*progress*
prot-	first	*prototype*
re-	again	*reappear*
retro-	back	*retrofit*
semi-	half, partly	*semicircle*
sub-	under	*submarine*
super-	more than	*supermarket*
syn-, sym-	together	*symbol*
trans-	across	*transatlantic*

(continued)

TABLE 3.4 ● *(continued)*

Prefix(es)	Meaning(s)	Sample Word
ultra-	beyond, extremely	*ultraconservative*
un-	not	*unwilling*
with-	against	*withhold*

TABLE 3.5 ● *Commonly Used Suffixes*

Suffix(es)	Meaning/Purpose	Sample Word
-able, -ible	can be done	*comfortable*
-al, -ial	relating to	*personal*
-arium	place of	*solarium*
-ation, -ition, -ion, -tion	act, process of	*animation*
-dom	quality, state	*freedom*
-ed	forms past tense for verb	*voted*
-en	made of	*wooden*
-er, est	indicates comparison	*harder*
-er	one who	*dancer*
-ful	full of	*hopeful*
-ic	relating to	*characteristic*
-ile	quality, state	*juvenile*
-ing	forms present participle	*hopping*
-ism	quality, state	*racism*
-ist	one who practices	*zoologist*
-ity, -ty	state of	*infinity*
-ive, -itive, -ative	adjective form of noun	*quantitative*
-less	without	*homeless*
-ly	characteristic of	*happily*
-ment	action, process	*excitement*
-ness	condition of	*sadness*
-ology	study of	*biology*
-ous, -eous, -ious	quality, state	*joyous*
-s, -es	forms plural of verb	*desks*
-tion	quality, state	*preservation*
-ular	relating to	*cellular*
-y	characterized by	*jumpy*

TABLE 3.6 ● *Commonly Used Word Roots*

Root	Meaning(s)	Sample Word
anthropo	man	*anthropology*
astro	star	*astronaut*
bio	life	*biology*
cardio	heart	*cardiac*
cede	go	*precede*
chromo	color	*chromatology*
demos	people	*democracy*
derma	skin	*epidermis*
dyna	power	*dynamic*
geo	earth	*geology*
helio	sun	*heliotrope*
hydro	water	*hydroponics*
hypno	sleep	*hypnosis*
ject	throw	*eject*
magni	great, big	*magnify*
man(u)	hand	*manuscript*
mono	one	*monoplane*
ortho	straight	*orthodox*
pod	foot	*pseudopod*
psycho	mind	*psychology*
pyro	fire	*pyrometer*
script	write	*manuscript*
terra	earth	*terrace*
thermo	heat	*thermometer*
zoo	animal	*zoology*

Word study is essential to learning. According to Harris and Hodges (1995), word study includes practice in word identification, as well as structural analysis, spelling, and vocabulary building. Structural analysis is especially important when teaching word study in grades 6–8. Bloodgood and Pacifici (2004) concur and add that "upper-level word study focuses on the structure and meaning of words by drawing students' attention to spelling patterns and word roots" (p. 250). The hands-on nature of word study—including analysis of the structures and features of words—motivates students to move beyond memorizing new words and think at higher levels.

Teaching Vocabulary in the Common Core Classroom

VOCABULARY LESSONS BENEFIT STUDENTS MOST WHEN THEY ARE designed as rich instructional tasks that address multiple Common Core State Standards. For example, a lesson based on learning vocabulary in an informational text might incorporate the standards listed in Table 3.7.

We can incorporate a variety of vocabulary-based strategies in our lessons. The following sections describe effective strategies and provide examples of their use in the classroom.

Semantic Question Map   The Semantic Question Map (McLaughlin, 2010) is a graphic organizer that contributes to students' understanding of a *focus word,* which appears in the center oval of the organizer. Multiple oval satellites extend from the center oval, and each satellite contains a question to prompt student responses. As students offer responses, they are recorded under the appropriate question. The completed organizer can be used to facilitate oral or written summaries. Figure 3.1 shows a completed Semantic Question Map about climate change.

Context Clues   Context clues are words surrounding an unknown word that help us determine the word's meaning. There are six different kinds of context clues: definition, example/illustration, comparison/contrast, logic, cause/effect, and mood/tone. Using context clues is a valuable strategy for determining word meanings. Figure 3.2 shows a

TABLE 3.7 ● *Examples of Integrating the Common Core State Standards in a Rich Instructional Task*

- **Reading Informational Text Standard 1:** to support students' analyzing what the text says
- **Reading Informational Text Standard 2:** to support students' determining central ideas and supporting details
- **Writing Standard 2:** to support students' engaging in clear and coherent informational writing about what they have read
- **Speaking and Listening Standard 1:** to encourage various types of discussion
- **Speaking and Listening Standard 5:** to address using multiple types of media in the lesson
- **Language Standard 2:** to support spelling as a key convention in student writing
- **Language Standard 4:** to address determining and clarifying word meanings
- **Language Standard 6:** to focus on using academic or grade-appropriate general vocabulary

FIGURE 3.1 ● Completed Semantic Question Map about Climate Change

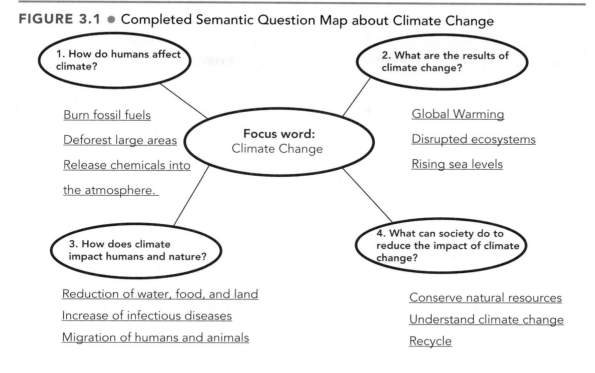

1. How do humans affect climate?

Burn fossil fuels

Deforest large areas

Release chemicals into

the atmosphere.

Focus word: Climate Change

2. What are the results of climate change?

Global Warming

Disrupted ecosystems

Rising sea levels

3. How does climate impact humans and nature?

Reduction of water, food, and land

Increase of infectious diseases

Migration of humans and animals

4. What can society do to reduce the impact of climate change?

Conserve natural resources

Understand climate change

Recycle

FIGURE 3.2 ● Completed Graphic Organizer for Recording Context Clues in *The Outsiders*

Unknown Word	Page	Part of Speech	Possible Meaning	Quote from Text
unfathomable	12	adjective	unable to understand	"He liked fights, blondes, and for some unfathomable reason, school."
roguishly	22	adverb	in a dishonest or mischievous way	"Dally grinned roguishly."
incredulous	24	adjective	not believable	"She gave him an incredulous look and then she threw her Coke in his face."

(continued)

FIGURE 3.2 ● *(continued)*

Unknown Word	Page	Part of Speech	Possible Meaning	Quote from Text
dumbfounded	39	adjective	astonished or confused	"Two-Bit and Johnny were staring at me now. 'No . . .' Two-Bit said, dumbfounded."
winced	39	verb	shrank back or hovered in fear	"Johnny's eyes went round and he winced as though I'd belted him."
passionately	40	adverb	with intense feeling	"It ain't fair! I cried passionately."
soused	43	adjective	drunk	"I think I'm a little soused."
misery	47	noun	extreme emotional distress and unhappiness	"Shoot," I said, startled out of my misery, "you got the whole gang."

completed graphic organizer that was used to record information about context clues for words in the young-adult novel *The Outsiders* (Hinton, 1967/2003).

Vocabulary Bookmark   When using Vocabulary Bookmark (McLaughlin & Allen, 2009), students self-select a word for the class to discuss. They also record what they think the word means and the page on which and the paragraph in which the word appears in the text. Figure 3.3 shows a completed Vocabulary Bookmark based on the term *greenhouse gases*.

Discipline-Specific Word Wall   Another teaching idea that supports students' learning and use of vocabulary is the Discipline-Specific Word Wall. This type of word wall should be displayed in classrooms for disciplinary courses (e.g., mathematics, science, and social studies) for two key purposes: to provide students with ready access to terminology and to illuminate the correct spelling of each term. Figure 3.4 presents a Discipline-Specific Word Wall in an algebra class.

In the Common Core Classroom

Adelina is a sixth-grade English language arts (ELA) teacher at a middle school. Her district has sponsored professional learning communities (PLCs) related to the CCSS for

FIGURE 3.3 ● Completed Vocabulary Bookmark for the Term *Greenhouse Gases*

Name _____

Vocabulary Bookmark

A word I think the whole class needs to talk about is

greenhouse gases

I think it means gas in the atmosphere that absorbs and releases heat from the earth.

Page 9

Paragraph 4

FIGURE 3.4 ● Sample Discipline-Specific Word Wall for an Algebra Class

Key Vocabulary

binomial	exponent	term
coefficient	expression	trinomial
constant	monomial	variable
equation	polynomial	

more than a year, and she has worked extensively with colleagues in implementing the standards—particularly ELA teachers in grades 6, 7, and 8.

One of the focal points of Adelina's PLC is integrating the vocabulary expectations of the language arts strands—Reading, Writing, Speaking and Listening, and Language—across the curriculum. To meet this goal, she decided to create a series of lessons containing rich instructional tasks in which vocabulary was a focus. These lessons were part of an integrated theme on the topic of *survival*. In planning the lessons, Adelina chose to use the Guided Comprehension five-step model for explicit strategy instruction: (1) explain, (2) demonstrate, (3) guide, (4) practice, and (5) reflect

(McLaughlin & Allen, 2009). In addition, she aligned her lessons with the following Common Core State Standards:

- **Reading Literature Standard 1:** Cite textual evidence.
- **Reading Literature Standard 2:** Determine the theme and details.
- **Reading Literature Standard 4:** Determine the meanings of words and phrases.
- **Writing Standard 3:** Write narratives to develop real or imagined events.
- **Writing Standard 4:** Produce clear and coherent writing.
- **Writing Standard 5:** Develop and strengthen writing with guidance and support.
- **Writing Standard 6:** Use technology to produce and publish writing.
- **Writing Standard 10:** Write routinely for both short and extended time periods.
- **Speaking and Listening Standard 1:** Engage in various types of discussions.
- **Speaking and Listening Standard 5:** Use multiple types of media in lessons.
- **Language Standard 2:** Use correct spelling as a convention of writing.
- **Language Standard 4:** Determine and clarify word meanings.
- **Language Standard 6:** Use both academic and grade-appropriate general vocabulary.

The lesson that follows is designed for grade 6 and focuses on word study—particularly, synonyms and parts of speech. The featured student texts are two young-adult novels: *Hatchet,* by Gary Paulsen (1977), and *Call It Courage,* by Armstrong Sperry (1941/1990). The lesson appears in Adelina's words and features student examples.

STAGE ONE

Teacher-Directed, Whole-Group Instruction

Text: **Hatchet** (Paulsen, 1987)

Explain: I began by asking students to brainstorm different parts of speech. We created a list on the board that included nouns, verbs, adjectives, adverbs, prepositions, and participles. Then, the students defined and gave examples of each part of speech, and I recorded their responses on the board.

Next, I explained to the students that we would be writing a type of form poem that required using different parts of speech. I said, "Today we will be creating cinquains. I wrote "c-i-n-q-u-a-i-n" on the board and said, "This is how *cinquain* is spelled, but it is pronounced 'sin-kane.' A cinquain is a type of form poem that requires us to write specific parts of speech in each line."

FIGURE 3.5 ● Cinquain Format

_____

One-word noun

_____ _____

Two adjectives describing line 1

_____ _____ _____

"ing" words telling actions of line 1

_____ _____ _____ _____

Four-word phrase describing a feeling related to line 1

_____

One-word synonym or reference to line 1

Then I used a PowerPoint presentation that contained a cinquain blackline and began to explain the format:

> The first line asks for a *noun*. On our review list, it says that a noun names a person, place, or thing. It also says that *teacher, school,* and *book* are some examples of nouns. So, when we're choosing a noun for line 1, we're really choosing the topic of our cinquain.
>
> The second line asks for two *adjectives* that describe the noun. On our review list, we said that adjectives describe nouns or other adjectives. Our examples of adjectives and the nouns they described include *green (light), happy (family),* and *deserted (house)*. So, in line 2, we will need to write two adjectives that describe the noun we chose for line 1.
>
> The third line asks for three -*ing* words that describe the action of the noun in line 1. On our review list, we said that participles end in -*ing* and they can describe nouns. Our examples of participles and the nouns they describe include *running (man), flying (football),* and *leaping (dancer)*.
>
> The fourth line is a four-word *phrase* that describes a feeling related to line 1. We didn't discuss phrases in our part of speech review, but we did talk about *prepositions*. How can we relate prepositions to our need for phrases?

In response to my question, Sam gave this answer: "Prepositions start prepositional phrases. So, if our preposition was *on,* we could say 'on a basketball court' is a prepositional phrase." I confirmed Sam's response, saying that prepositions do begin prepositional phrases and noting that his example was correct. Then I returned to my explanation:

> Let's take a look at the prepositions on our list. We have *in, by,* and *through.* What are some samples of prepositional phrases we can create using these prepositions?

Students responses included "in our backyard," "by the blue car," and "through the parking lot." I explained that they had offered good examples. Then Chrissanna said, "Aren't there other kinds of phrases? Sometimes when we write ideas, but they're not complete sentences, you say they're *phrases*." I answered Chrissanna's question as follows:

> That's correct. When we write ideas that are not complete sentences—something is missing, such as a subject or verb—that is also a phrase. In our cinquains, we can write any kind of phrase, as long as it describes a feeling relating to the noun we write in line 1.

Once again, I returned to explaining the cinquain format:

> The fifth and final line is a one-word synonym for the noun in line 1. We know that *synonyms* are words that mean the same or nearly the same thing, so this word must be a synonym for the word we write in line 1. Let's notice that the first line requires that we write a noun and the last line requires that we write its synonym. So, a cinquain is a form poem about synonyms.
>
> There are many ways to approach writing a cinquain, but it is sometimes easier to write this form poem by completing the first and last lines before completing the others.

Demonstrate: To demonstrate, I used a read-aloud, a Think-Aloud, and the cinquain blackline. I began by reading aloud Chapter 9 of *Hatchet,* by Gary Paulsen (1987). I explained to the students that I would choose the noun that would be the topic of our cinquain from this chapter. Then I used a think-aloud as I began writing the cinquain:

> This chapter is about Brian trying to start a fire, so I'm going to make *fire* the topic of our cinquain. I am going to write *fire* on the first line, where it says *Noun,* because that is the subject of my poem and I know that a subject is always a noun.
>
> Next, I need two adjectives for *fire.* Who can remind us what an adjective does?

Benjamin responded, "It describes a noun or another adjective." I confirmed that Benjamin's definition was correct and then continued with my think-aloud:

> The first word that I'm thinking of to describe *fire* is *hot,* so I will write that on the first blank. Another word I'm thinking of to describe *fire* is *bright,* so I will write that on the second blank. So, the two adjectives I wrote in line 2 are *hot* and *bright.*
>
> Now, I need to think about the third line. I need to write three *-ing* words that describe the action of *fire.* What part of speech are *-ing* words?

Julianne said, "They are participles." I confirmed her response and continued the think-aloud:

> A participle that comes to mind is *flaming,* so I will write that on the first blank on line 3.

Guide: Next, I guided the students to work in pairs to complete the two blanks in line 3 of the cinquain. After the partners offered their suggestions, I wrote *sparking* and *cracking* in the blanks on line 3.

Practice: Students practiced by completing lines 4 and 5 of the cinquain with their partners. Then they shared their responses with the whole group. We selected responses to complete our cinquain, and then we read our completed poem:

Fire

Hot Bright

Flaming Sparking Cracking

Light and Heat Provider

Inferno

Reflect: As a class, we reflected on how we can use the cinquain form poem to review certain parts of speech and summarize concepts. The students thought it was fun to manipulate the parts of speech to make them fit into the necessary lines and number of spaces. For example, Jeffrey said, "I knew that a fire made sparks, so I changed *sparks* into *sparking* in order to use the word in line 3."

STAGE TWO

Teacher-Guided, Small-Group Instruction

Text: *Call It Courage* (Sperry, 1941/1990) (Texts should be varied according to the students' abilities.)

Review: To review, we revisited the cinquain form. We also briefly discussed the parts of speech we had brainstormed and listed in Stage 1 and gave examples of each. I explained that we would continue to use the cinquain form to practice using these parts of speech and that we would choose the topic for another cinquain after reading the first chapter of *Call It Courage,* by Armstrong Sperry (1941/1990). Then I distributed copies of the cinquain blackline to students.

Guide: I guided students to partner-read Chapter 1, prompting as necessary. After we discussed the events of the chapter, I asked students to think of a noun that could be the topic of our cinquain. As a class, we decided on the word *sea,* because that is the focus of the first chapter.

After writing the word *sea* on line 1 of their blacklines, the students worked together to think of adjectives to describe the sea. I suggested that they close their eyes, visualize the sea, and think of words to describe it. Liza asked if they could use words from the chapter, and I told her that was a great idea. The students chose *stormy* and *calm*—words the author used to describe the sea at different times.

Practice: To practice, students worked in pairs to complete the remaining lines of the blackline. When each pair had completed their cinquain, they shared the poem with the rest of the class.

Reflect: The students commented that writing a cinquain form poem was a fun way to practice using parts of speech correctly. They also thought using the form was a great way to write poetry. Silvio said, "I like writing form poems. They tell us what kinds of words to put where they need to be. This makes poem writing easier and more fun for me."

Student-Facilitated Comprehension Centers

Make-a Book Center: Students wrote and illustrated cinquains on theme-related topics as pages for *Our Class Book of Cinquains*. Most students decided to use computers to create their pages.

Theme Center: Students self-selected texts from numerous leveled titles I had placed at this center. Then they wrote cinquains using theme-related topics.

Student-Facilitated Comprehension Routines

Literature Circles: We adapted the Literature Circle so that students wrote cinquains as an extension activity. They based their cinquains on topics from the novels they were reading and shared their poems with the other members of their groups.

Cross-Age Reading Experiences: Students read texts with their fourth grade cross-age partners and wrote and illustrated cinquains together.

STAGE THREE

Teacher-Facilitated, Whole-Group Reflection and Goal Setting

Share: In small groups, students shared the cinquains they wrote in Stage Two. After sharing in small groups, some students volunteered to read their poems to the whole group.

Reflect: Once again, the students noted how writing cinquains helped them to practice using different parts of speech correctly. They all agreed that this was a fun way to write poetry and to review and practice parts of speech.

Set New Goals: We decided that we were comfortable writing cinquains and that we wanted to learn to write other types of form poetry, such as diamantes.

Assessment Options

I used formative assessment, including my own observations and students' cinquains and reflections. When working with students with disabilities, I was careful to put a different colored dot at the start of each line on the cinquain blackline, so that I could easily draw the students' attention to a particular line. In guided settings, I assigned volunteer "scribes," as needed, to help students with disabilities record their ideas on the blackline. In practice settings, I enlarged the cinquain blackline, so that students could more easily record their responses.

When working with English language learners, I provided supports, such as pictures and a brief preteaching session. I also provided sufficient wait time and encouraged discussion. When appropriate, I paired English language learners with native English speakers and integrated information about their cultures as class resources. I assessed English language learners' performance both orally and in written format and paid close attention to their illustrations, checking for poem–picture matches.

Ensuring that our students are knowledgeable about words is essential to their meeting all of the vocabulary-related expectations of the Common Core. It is also a vital component in their preparations to become college and career ready.

REFERENCES

Baumann, J. F., & Kame'enui, E. J. (1991). Research on vocabulary instruction: Ode to Voltaire. In J. Flood, J. M. Jensen, D. Lapp, & J. R. Squire (Eds.), *Handbook on teaching the English language arts* (pp. 604–632). New York, NY: Macmillan.

Beck, I. L., & McKeown, M. G. (1991). Conditions of vocabulary acquisition. In R. Barr, M. Kamil, P. Mosenthal, & P. D. Pearson (Eds.), *Handbook of reading research* (Vol. 2, pp. 789–814). White Plains, NY: Longman.

Beck, I. L., McKeown, M. G., & Kucan, L. (2002). *Bringing words to life: Robust vocabulary instruction*. New York, NY: Guilford Press.

Beck, I. L., McKeown, M. G., & Kucan, L. (2008). *Creating robust vocabulary: Frequently asked questions & extended examples*. New York, NY: Guilford Press.

Blachowicz, C. L., & Fisher, P. (2000). Vocabulary instruction. In M. L. Kamil, P. B. Mosenthal, P. D. Pearson, & R. Barr (Eds.), *Handbook of reading research* (Vol. 3, pp. 503–523). Mahwah, NJ: Erlbaum.

Blachowicz, C. L., Fisher, P., Ogle, D. M., & Watts-Taffe, S. (2006). Vocabulary: Questions from the classroom. *Reading Research Quarterly, 41*(4), 524–539.

Blachowicz, C. L. Z., Fisher, P. J. L., & Watts-Taffe, S. (2011). Teaching vocabulary: Leading edge research and practice. In T. V. Rasinski (Ed.). *Rebuilding the foundation: Effective reading instruction for 21st century literacy* (pp. 203–222). Bloomington, IN: Solution Tree Press.

Blachowicz, C. L., & Lee, J. J. (1991). Vocabulary development in the whole literacy classroom. *The Reading Teacher, 45,* 188–195.

Bloodgood, J. W., & Pacifici, L. C. (2004). Bringing word study to intermediate classrooms. *The Reading Teacher, 58*(3), 250–263.

Dixon-Krauss, L. (2001/2002). Using literature as a context for teaching vocabulary. *Journal of Adolescent & Adult Literacy, 45*(4), 310–318.

Duke, N. (2007). *Comprehension throughout the day.* Paper presented at the Alaska State Literacy Conference, Anchorage, AK.

Graves, M. F. (2006). *The vocabulary book: Learning and instruction.* New York, NY: Teachers College Press.

Graves, M. F., & Watts-Taffe, S. M. (2002). The place of word consciousness in a research-based vocabulary program. In A. E. Farstrup & S. J. Samuels (Eds.), *What research has to say about reading instruction* (pp. 140–165). Newark, DE: International Reading Association.

Harris, T. L., & Hodges, R. E. (Eds.). (1995). *The literacy dictionary: The vocabulary of reading and writing.* Newark, DE: International Reading Association.

Hiebert, E. H., Pearson, P. D., Taylor, B. M., Richardson, V., & Paris, S. G. (1998). *Every child a reader.* Ann Arbor, MI: Center for the Improvement of Early Reading Achievement.

Kucan, L. (2012). What is most important to know about vocabulary? *The Reading Teacher, 65*(6), 360–366.

McLaughlin, M. (2010). *Content area reading: Teaching and learning in an age of multiple literacies.* Boston, MA: Allyn & Bacon.

McLaughlin, M., & Allen, M. B. (2009). *Guided comprehension in grades 3–8.* Newark, DE: International Reading Association.

National Governors Association Center for Best Practices & Council of Chief State School Officers (NGA & CCSSO). (2010). *Common Core State Standards: English language arts and literacy in history/social studies, science, and technical subjects.* Washington, DC: Authors. Retrieved from www.corestandards.org/assets/CCSSI_ELA%20Standards.pdf.

National Institute of Child Health and Human Development (NICHD). (2000).

National Reading Panel. (2000). *Teaching children to read: An evidence-based assessment of the scientific research literature on reading and its implications for reading instruction.* Washington, DC: National Institutes of Health.

Pearson, P. D., Hiebert, E. H, & Kamil, M. L. (2007). Vocabulary assessment: What we know and what we need to learn. *Reading Research Quarterly, 42,* 282–296.

Richek, M. A. (2005). Words are wonderful: Interactive, time-efficient strategies to teach meaning vocabulary. *The Reading Teacher, 58*(5), 414–423.

Snow, C. E., Burns, M. S., & Griffin, P. G. (Eds.). (1998). *Preventing reading difficulties in young children.* Washington, DC: National Academy Press.

LITERATURE CITED

Hinton, S. E. (1997). *The outsiders.* New York, NY: Puffin Books. (Original work published 1967)

Paulsen, G. (1987). *Hatchet.* New York, NY: Bradbury Press.

Sperry, A. (1990). *Call it courage.* New York, NY: Aladdin//Simon & Schuster. (Original work published 1941)

Text Complexity and Close Reading

WHAT CAN WE DO TO HELP OUR STUDENTS be successful in meeting the College and Career Readiness Anchor Standard and the Common Core State Standard (CSSS) for complex text? We obviously need to understand the expectations of the CCR Standards and the CCSS, but we also need to understand how to teach reading. As noted in previous chapters, the writers of the CCSS delineated key expectations for students of various grade levels. However, they have left the teaching in the hands of the educators. This is a particularly salient point when it comes to teaching reading and using complex texts.

Monkey Business/Fotolia

Our goal in this chapter is to situate the CCSS within the theory and practice involved in reading complex text. We will discuss the knowledge and skills students need to know and be able to demonstrate to meet the expectations of the standards.

This chapter is divided into several main sections. To begin, we outline what is known about the nature of complex text. Then, we examine reading complex texts as an expectation of the CCSS. Next, we explore aspects of literacy that support the teaching of complex texts, and define and discuss the terms *reading closely* and *close reading*. (The latter is a literary analysis technique that American College Testing (ACT) is promoting for reading complex text.) Finally, we consider reflections from several classroom teachers as they think through how they will teach their students to read complex text.

Understanding Text Complexity

SINCE THE ADVENT OF THE CCSS, THE TOPIC of *text complexity* has been met with serious inquiry. In fact, however, contemplating the complex nature of text is not new to individuals who teach reading (Pearson & Hiebert, 2012). Literacy professionals are very knowledgeable about text and fully understand its multifaceted features. As Hiebert (2012) has observed:

> The complexity of a text is a function of the reader's proficiency. There are complex beginning reading texts, there are complex middle-grade texts, etc. Numerous features can make a text complex. Typically, complex texts have complex ideas and, usually, those ideas are conveyed with rare and infrequent vocabulary.

In 2006, ACT established three levels of increasingly complex texts: uncomplicated, more challenging, and complex. ACT further delineated the characteristics of texts along a continuum of complexity, as follows:

- **Relationships** (interactions among ideas or characters)
- **Richness** (amount and sophistication of information conveyed through data or literary devices)
- **Structure** (how the text is organized and how it progresses)
- **Style** (author's tone and use of language)
- **Vocabulary** (author's word choice)
- **Purpose** (author's intent in writing the text) (ACT, 2006, p. 14)

Although several of these characteristics are rooted more in literary analysis than in reading, the three categories defined by ACT (uncomplicated, more challenging, and complex) strongly parallel the terms used by literacy professionals to describe levels of text: independent, instructional, and frustration. Students can read *independent-level texts* with no assistance, and they can read *instructional-level texts* with some assistance from the teacher. Students cannot read *frustration-level texts,* and so these texts are often shared with students in other ways, including teacher read-alouds and books on CD.

Including text complexity in the College and Career Readiness (CCR) Anchor Standards and the CCSS in no way ensures that students can or will be able to read complex text. The teaching of reading is built on the premise that teaching should take place at the student's instructional level. This includes the use of instructional-level texts. Further, in reading instruction, students read independent-level texts without teacher assistance when engaged in pursuits such as practicing skills (e.g., fluency) and strategies (e.g., summarizing).

Shanahan, Fisher, and Frey (2012) suggest that when teachers understand what makes texts complex, they are better prepared to teach students how to read them. Shanahan et al. further note that multiple factors determine the complexity of a text: vocabulary, sentence structure, coherence (i.e., connecting ideas across text), organization, and background knowledge.

The Common Core and Complex Text

THE CCSS ARE DESIGNED WITH THE EXPECTATION that students will build their understanding of increasingly complex texts. This is specifically noted in the CCR Anchor Standards for Reading, where Standard 10 in the cluster Range of Reading and Level of Text Complexity states, "Read and comprehend complex literary and informational texts independently and proficiently" (CCSSO & NGA, 2010a, p. 35). Text complexity is further addressed in the CCSS Reading standards, which build on CCR Anchor Standard 10 and address particular types of text. Table 4.1 presents Standard 10 from the CCSS Reading Standards for Literature for grades 6–8, and Table 4.2 presents Standard 10 from the CCSS Reading Standards for Informational Text for the same grades.

TABLE 4.1 ● *Common Core State Standards for Reading Literature: Standard 10, Grades 6–8*

Grade 6 Students	Grade 7 Students	Grade 8 Students
Range of Reading and Text Complexity		
10. By the end of the year, read and comprehend literature, including stories, dramas, and poems, in the grades 6–8 text complexity band proficiently, with scaffolding as needed at the high end of the range.	10. By the end of the year, read and comprehend literature, including stories, dramas, and poems, in the grades 6–8 text complexity band proficiently, with scaffolding as needed at the high end of the range.	10. By the end of the year, read and comprehend literature, including stories, dramas, and poems, at the high end of grades 6–8 text complexity band independently and proficiently.

TABLE 4.2 ● *Common Core State Standards for Reading Informational Text: Standard 10, Grades 6–8*

Grade 6 Students	Grade 7 Students	Grade 8 Students
Range of Reading and Text Complexity		
10. By the end of the year, read and comprehend literary nonfiction in the grades 6–8 text complexity band proficiently, with scaffolding as needed at the high end of the range.	10. By the end of the year, read and comprehend literary nonfiction in the grades 6–8 text complexity band proficiently, with scaffolding as needed at the high end of the range.	10. By the end of the year, read and comprehend literary nonfiction at the high end of the grades 6–8 text complexity band independently and proficiently.

Information about text complexity is also provided in Appendix A of the CCSS (NGA & CCSSO, 2010b, pp. 2–9). In this appendix, a discussion of issues regarding text complexity identifies two problematic trends: (1) reading texts have decreased in difficulty over the past 50 years and (2) students have lost the ability to read and analyze difficult text on their own. One of the reasons cited for students' lack of independent reading is reliance on teacher scaffolding. Appendix A also features a discussion of the research base that provides a rationale for increasing text complexity.

The CCSS provide a three-part model for measuring text complexity. It is featured both in the Standards and Appendix A (see Figure 4.1). As outlined in both Appendix A (NGA & CCSSO, 2010b, p. 4) and the CCSS document (NGA & CCSSO, 2010a, p. 57), text complexity consists of three equally important elements:

1. **Qualitative dimensions** of text complexity can be measured only by an attentive human reader and include concepts such as levels of meaning or purpose, the way the text is structured, the clarity and conventional nature of the language, and the types of knowledge demands the text makes on the reader. Qualitative dimensions relate to the kinds of background knowledge that any reader must have to comprehend the text (e.g., text structure, vocabulary, and language).

2. **Quantitative dimensions** of text complexity are typically measured by computer software and include components such as word length and frequency, sentence length, and text cohesion. Quantitative dimensions relate to the measured reading level of a text. (The CCSS specifically provide text levels as measured by Lexiles.)

3. **Reader and task considerations** involve evaluations of the appropriateness of a given text for a given student. These evaluations are made by teachers employing their professional judgment, experience, and knowledge of the student and the subject. Reader and task considerations relate to knowing an individual student's abilities,

FIGURE 4.1 ● Three-Part Model of Text Complexity

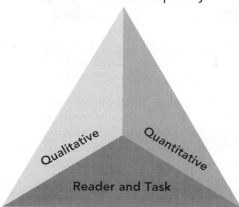

experiences, interests, and possible motivation for reading a particular text before making a determination that the text is appropriate for a student.

The CCSS include expectations that students will read complex text. However, we may question whether having students read such texts is worthwhile when we examine the rubrics created by the CCSS to measure text complexity. The Text Complexity Qualitative Measures Rubric for Literary Text and the Text Complexity Qualitative Measures Rubric for Informational Text are featured in Figures 4.2 and 4.3. In characterizing text at the high level of complexity, the rubrics describe the quality of *conventionality* as the "heavy use of abstract and/or figurative language or irony" and the quality of *clarity* as "generally unfamiliar, archaic, domain-specific, and/or academic language; dense and complex; may be ambiguous or purposefully misleading."

These descriptions of the characteristics of complex text have left literacy professionals wanting. It is one thing to expect students to read at grade level, but individuals who know about literacy understand that not all students will meet the expectations of the CCSS. However, it is quite another thing to expect students to construct meaning from a text that is described as "abstract, archaic, dense, ambiguous, and purposefully misleading." (It is important to note that the text complexity rubrics for lower grade levels describe complex text in more appealing terms.)

The difficulty in supporting the CCSS description of the structure of complex text is illuminated by another text complexity document produced by the creators of the standards: *Suggested Considerations for Reader and Task* (NGA & CCSSO, 2010d). This

FIGURE 4.2 ● Text Complexity: Qualitative Measures Rubric—Literary Text, Grades 6–8

Text Title: _____ Text Author: _____

MEANING			
High	**Middle High**	**Middle Low**	**Low**
Multiple levels/layers of complex meaning	Multiple levels/layers of meaning	Single level/layer of complex meaning	Single level/layer of simple meaning

STRUCTURE			
High	**Middle High**	**Middle Low**	**Low**
Narrative Structure: complex, implicit, and unconventional	**Narrative Structure:** some complexities, more implicit than explicit, some unconventionality	**Narrative Structure:** largely simple structure, more explicit than implicit, largely conventional	**Narrative Structure:** simple, explicit, conventional
Narration: many shifts in point of view	**Narration:** occasional shifts in point of view	**Narration:** few, if any, shifts in point of view	**Narration:** no shifts in point of view
Order of Events: frequent manipulations of time and sequence (not in chronological order)	**Order of Events:** several major shifts in time, use of flashback	**Order of Events:** occasional use of flashback, no major shifts in time	**Order of Events:** chronological

LANGUAGE			
High	**Middle High**	**Middle Low**	**Low**
Conventionality: heavy use of abstract and/or figurative language or irony	**Conventionality:** contains abstract and/or figurative language or irony	**Conventionality:** subtle use of figurative language or irony	**Conventionality:** little or no use of figurative language or irony
Clarity: generally unfamiliar, archaic, domain-specific, and/or academic language; dense and complex; may be ambiguous or purposefully misleading	**Clarity:** somewhat complex language that is occasionally unfamiliar, archaic, domain-specific, or overly academic	**Clarity:** largely contemporary, familiar, conversational language that is explicit and literal; rarely unfamiliar, archaic, domain-specific, or overly academic	**Clarity:** contemporary, familiar, conversational language that is explicit and literal; easy-to-understand

(continued)

FIGURE 4.2 ● (*continued*)

KNOWLEDGE DEMANDS			
High	**Middle High**	**Middle Low**	**Low**
Life Experiences: explores multiple complex, sophisticated themes; multiple perspectives presented; experiences portrayed are not fantasy but are distinctly different to the common reader	**Life Experiences:** explores multiple themes of varying levels of complexity; experiences portrayed are not fantasy but are uncommon to most readers	**Life Experiences:** explores a single complex theme; experiences portrayed are common to many readers or are clearly fantasy	**Life Experiences:** explores a single theme; single perspective presented and everyday experiences are portrayed that are common to most readers or experiences are clearly fantasy
Cultural/Literary Knowledge: requires an extensive depth of literary/cultural knowledge; many references/allusions to other texts and/or cultural elements	**Cultural/Literary Knowledge:** requires moderate levels of cultural/literary knowledge; some references/allusions to other texts and/or cultural elements	**Cultural/Literary Knowledge:** requires some cultural/literary knowledge; few references/allusions to other texts and/or cultural elements	**Cultural/Literary Knowledge:** requires only common, everyday cultural/literary knowledge; no references/allusions to other texts and/or cultural elements

FIGURE 4.3 ● Text Complexity: Qualitative Measures Rubric—Informational Text, Grades 6–8

Text Title: _____ Text Author: _____

PURPOSE			
High	**Middle High**	**Middle Low**	**Low**
Complex, implied, and/or difficult to determine; may have multiple purposes	Implied, but can be inferred; may have multiple purposes	Implied, but easy to identify based on context	Explicitly stated

(continued)

FIGURE 4.3 ● *(continued)*

STRUCTURE			
High	**Middle High**	**Middle Low**	**Low**
Organization: highly complex; implicit connections between ideas; conforms to the conventions of a specific content area or discipline	**Organization:** complex; some explicit connections between ideas; may exhibit traits common to a specific content area or discipline	**Organization:** may be complex; largely explicit connections between ideas; generally follows the conventions of the genre	**Organization:** simple; explicit connections between ideas; conforms to the conventions of the genre
Text Features: if used, are essential in understanding content	**Text Features:** if used, greatly enhance the reader's understanding of content	**Text Features:** if used, enhance the reader's understanding of content	**Text Features:** if used, help the reader navigate and understand content but are not essential
Use of Graphics: if used, interpretation of complex graphics essential to understanding the text; may also provide information not conveyed in the text*	**Use of Graphics:** if used, some graphics are complex and may occasionally be essential to the understanding of the text	**Use of Graphics:** if used, graphics are mostly simple and supplementary to understanding the text	**Use of Graphics:** if used, graphics are simple and unnecessary to understanding the text
LANGUAGE			
High	**Middle High**	**Middle Low**	**Low**
Conventionality: contains abstract and/or figurative language or irony	**Conventionality:** occasionally contains abstract and/or figurative language or irony	**Conventionality:** largely contemporary, conversational language	**Conventionality:** contemporary, conversational language
Clarity: dense and complex language that is generally unfamiliar, archaic, discipline-specific, or overly academic; language may be ambiguous or purposefully misleading	**Clarity:** somewhat complex language that is occasionally unfamiliar, archaic, discipline-specific, or overly academic	**Clarity:** largely explicit, familiar language; easy-to-understand and rarely archaic, discipline-specific, or overly academic	**Clarity:** clear, explicit, literal, easy-to-understand language

(continued)

FIGURE 4.3 ● (*continued*)

KNOWLEDGE DEMANDS			
High	**Middle High**	**Middle Low**	**Low**
Subject Matter Knowledge: requires extensive, perhaps specialized or even theoretical discipline-specific content knowledge	**Subject Matter Knowledge:** requires moderate levels of discipline-specific content knowledge; some theoretical knowledge may enhance understanding	**Subject Matter Knowledge:** everyday, practical knowledge is largely necessary; requires some discipline-specific content knowledge	**Subject Matter Knowledge:** requires only everyday, practical knowledge and familiarity with conventions of the genre
Intertextuality: many references to/ citations of other texts or outside ideas, theories, etc.	**Intertextuality:** some references to/ citations of other texts or outside ideas, theories, etc.	**Intertextuality:** few references to/ citations of other texts or outside ideas, theories, etc.	**Intertextuality:** no references to/ citations of other texts or outside ideas, theories, etc.

Note: Many books for the youngest students rely heavily on graphics to convey meaning and are an exception to this generalization.

document, which addresses the third element in the model for measuring text complexity, raises queries related to these specific aspects of literacy:

- cognitive capabilities, including paying attention, making connections, and applying higher-level thinking skills
- reading skills, such as comprehension strategies
- motivation and engagement with the task and the text, including purpose, interest, and engagement
- prior knowledge and engagement, such as having adequate prior knowledge about the topic, making explicit connections, and having prior knowledge of the vocabulary and genre
- content and theme, including concerns such as reader comfort and maturity
- complexity of associated tasks, such as addressing whether the complexity of any activity associated with the task will interfere with the reading experience

The complete *Suggested Considerations for Reader and Task* is provided in Figure 4.4. As you read this document, keep in mind that it is the only CCSS document in which several literacy-related terms appear, including *prior knowledge, reading strategies,* and *motivation and engagement.*

FIGURE 4.4 ● Suggested Considerations for Reader and Task

Cognitive Capabilities

- Do readers at this grade level possess the necessary **attention** to read and comprehend the text?
- Will the readers at this grade level be able to **remember and make connections** among the various details presented in the text?
- Do readers at this grade level possess the necessary **critical/analytical thinking skills** to understand the relationships between the various parts of the text?
- Will the text help to develop the **attention, memory,** and **critical/analytic thinking skills** necessary for future reading endeavors?

Reading Skills

- Do readers at this grade level possess the necessary **inferencing skills** to "read between the lines" and make connections among elements that may not be explicit in the text?
- Do readers at this grade level possess the necessary **visualization skills** to imagine what is occurring or what is being described in the text?
- Do readers at this grade level possess the necessary **questioning skills** to challenge the ideas being presented in this text and consider those ideas from multiple points of view?
- Do readers at this grade level possess the necessary **comprehension strategies** to manage this text?
- Will the text help to develop the **inferencing skills, visualization skills, questioning skills,** and **comprehension strategies** necessary for future reading endeavors?

Motivation and Engagement with Task and Text

- Will the readers at this grade level **understand the purpose**—which might shift over the course of the reading experience—for reading the text (i.e., skimming, studying to retain content, close reading, etc.)?
- Will the readers at this grade level be **interested in the content** of the text?
- Might the readers at this grade level **develop an interest in this content** because of this text?
- Do readers at this grade level believe that they will be able to read and understand the text?
- Will the readers at this grade level be **interested and engaged with the style of writing and the presentation of ideas** within the text?
- Will the text **maintain the reader's motivation and engagement** throughout the reading experience?

Prior Knowledge and Experience

- Do readers at this grade level possess **adequate prior knowledge and/or experience regarding the topic** of the text to manage the material that is presented?
- Are there any **explicit connections** that can be made between what content the readers at this grade level will encounter in the text and other learning that may occur in this or another class?

(continued)

FIGURE 4.4 ● *(continued)*

- Do readers at this grade level possess **adequate prior knowledge and/or experience regarding the vocabulary** used within the text to manage the material that is presented?
- Do readers at this grade level possess **adequate knowledge of and/or experience with the genre** of the text to manage the material that is presented?
- Do readers at this grade level possess **adequate knowledge of and/or experience with the language** (i.e. syntax, diction, rhetoric) of the text to manage the material that is presented?

Content and/or Theme Concerns

- Are there any **potentially concerning elements of content or theme** that might contribute to students, teachers, administrators, and/or parents feeling uncomfortable with reading the text?
- Do readers at this grade level possess the **maturity** to respond appropriately to any potentially concerning elements of content or theme?

Complexity of Associated Tasks

- Will the **complexity of any tasks** associated with the text interfere with the reading experience?
- Will the **complexity of any questions asked or discussed** concerning this text interfere with the reading experience?

Source: NGA & CCSSO, 2010d

Exemplar Texts

Appendix B of the CCSS (NGA & CCSSO, 2010c) provides a list of exemplar texts for each text complexity band. These are not required texts; rather, they are titles suggested for use in facilitating teachers' comparison of texts as they plan to use materials that represent the complexity deemed appropriate in the CCSS. For grades 6–8, literary texts include stories, poems, and plays and informational texts include works of literary nonfiction, not only for the English language arts but also for specific content areas (e.g., history/social studies, science, mathematics, and technical subjects).

The publication of the *Revised Publishers' Criteria for the Common Core State Standards in English Language Arts and Literacy* for grades K–2 and grades 3–12 (Coleman & Pimentel, 2012a, b) has sent publishers a clear message about the importance of complex texts in reading instruction. Even MetaMetrics (2012), the company responsible for the Lexile measurement system, is recalibrating its text-leveling system to align with the higher expectations of the CCSS. Clearly, the CCSS have established the need to focus on students' ability to read complex texts.

Reading Closely versus *Close Reading*

The CCSS use the term *reading closely* to describe focused, attentive reading, but ACT (2006) uses the term *close reading*. There is a difference between these terms. *Reading closely* involves seeking a deep comprehension of the text, which is the outcome of reading from a critical stance. *Close reading,* on the other hand, is not a reading method but rather a literary analysis technique used primarily by college students. We will examine the meanings and uses of both terms.

Reading Closely   In College and Career Readiness Standard 1, students are expected to:
     "Read closely to determine what the text says explicitly and to make logical inferences from it; cite specific textual evidence when writing or speaking to support conclusions drawn from the text." (NGA Center & CCSSO, 2010a, p. 10)
     The Aspen Institute (Brown & Kappes, 2012) suggests that reading closely is an instructional strategy in which teachers and students engage in a comprehensive literacy program, "Reading closely is a scaffolded process in which the teacher provides modeling and students engage in guided practice of the skills and strategies needed to independently read and comprehend increasingly complex text." (Brown & Kappes, 2012, p. 4). The goal is that each time the text is read, the depth of students' understanding increases.
     We can use this definition to teach students how to read closely. This type of instruction takes place in small groups and includes three readings of a short, complex text over multiple lessons. Discussion and notetaking permeate all three stages of reading closely and help students to refine their understanding. To begin, the teacher selects the text, ensuring that it is suitably complex, and guides students to analyze it. In the first reading, the teacher briefly activates prior knowledge and engages students in a literal read of the text, during which they respond to text-dependent questions. When the passage has been read, everyone discusses the text, noting personal meaning, vocabulary, and points that were confusing. During the second reading, students determine the author's purpose, raise questions, analyze text structure, and contemplate theme development. During the third reading, students examine multiple themes the author may be trying to convey and summarize their thinking across all three readings. Throughout this process, teachers gradually release responsibility to the students, from guiding students' reading of a text to students' reading closely independently with deep comprehension.

Close Reading   Proponents of close reading recommend that teachers should not provide background information about the text, engage students in prereading activities, or teach lessons in reading strategies. Instead, students should approach a text "cold" to glean what they can about the author's message and ideas. In a video explaining the concept of close reading (EngageNY, 2012), David Coleman dismisses the purpose of pre-reading with this statement: "Predicting what is in a text before reading it is not an essential college and career ready skill." Coleman also dismisses the idea of teaching so-called generic reading strategies before conducting a close reading of a complex text. Coleman's statements, as well as statements from other proponents of his views have sparked a debate over the use of prereading strategies in reading instruction (Gewertz, 2012). (It is also important to note that David Coleman is not, nor has he ever been, an educator.)

Such statements have the potential to negate decades of research on how to help students learn to read. Students who cannot read well enough to comprehend today's classroom materials are not going to magically have the skills needed to read and analyze complex text on their own. An unintended result of the Common Core State Reading standards that address complex text is that teachers are being asked to use close reading in place of traditional, research-based, explicit reading comprehension instruction. The use of close reading as a literary analysis technique does not support the social constructivist nature of reading.

When engaging in close reading, as defined by ACT and David Coleman, the reader uses subtle clues in the text to discern how the author presents ideas, makes intentional word choices, and conveys a message. When reading informational and argumentative text, the reader also looks for the author's claims and the evidence provided to support them.

Model lessons for close reading, beginning as early as first grade, are posted on websites such as Achieve the Core (Student Achievement Partners, 2013). These lessons are delivered in whole-class settings across multiple days and focus on reading brief complex texts. In the lessons, teachers are directed to limit before-reading discussion and instruction; consequently, there is no activation of students' background knowledge. Students read the text at least three times:

1. During the first reading, students read the text independently without any assistance. This is highly reminiscent of *cold reading,* a practice frequently used in the decades before reading came to be viewed as a social constructivist process.

2. The second reading comprises a read-aloud provided by the teacher or a competent peer. During this reading, there may be discussion of domain-specific vocabulary, context, or sentence structure. After the second reading, the teacher typically poses text-dependent questions and students use the text to find the answers.

3. In the third reading, students read the text and work alone or with partners to find evidence to answer the text-dependent questions.

In some of the model lessons, students engage in more extended vocabulary instruction or in an activity using art, music, drama, or graphic organizers to visualize parts of text. Most of the lessons end with each student developing a concise, single sentence to answer each teacher-dependent question and/or writing an analysis of the text supported by evidence from the text.

In 2012, the International Reading Association (IRA) published *Literacy Implementation Guidance for the ELA Common Core Standards.* One of the issues addressed in this document is text complexity, which is described in a section called "Use of Challenging Texts" (see Figure 4.5). The IRA makes the following suggestions about developing students' ability to read complex texts:

- Adding more challenging texts to the existing curriculum will not meet the expectations of the CCSS.

- To help students meet the expected end-of-year benchmarks established by the CCSS, teachers should provide a wide range of high-quality informational and narrative texts, including some that are easier than those specified in the standards.

- To ensure that students' interactions with such texts result in maximum learning, teachers should provide not only significantly more adroit instructional scaffolding but also scaffolding of a focused, purposeful nature, including rereading, explanation, encouragement, and other supports within lessons.

FIGURE 4.5 ● Literacy Implementation Guidance for the ELA Common Core Standards

Use of Challenging Texts

The CCSS require that students read more challenging texts during instruction than has been general practice in the past, and there is reason to believe that this shift could help students reach more advanced literacy achievement levels. But, research also shows this to be a complex instructional issue and one that will not likely be accomplished successfully without a nuanced and thoughtful approach. Merely adding more challenging texts to the curriculum will not be a sufficient or effective response to this requirement.

The Common Core State Standards specify the levels of text that students need to be able to read effectively by the *ends* of school years. This does not mean that all assigned reading should be at these levels, however. To help students to attain the necessary end-of-year levels, teachers need to establish an ambitious itinerary of rich and varied informational and narrative texts, including some texts that are easier than the Standards specify. Athletes vary their routines to build strength, flexibility, and stamina; likewise, readers need reading experiences with a range of text difficulties and lengths if they are to develop these characteristics as readers.

Finally, beyond the beginning reading levels, the CCSS guidelines on text complexity encourage teachers to place students in at least some texts that they are likely to struggle with in terms of fluency and reading comprehension. This represents a major shift in instructional approach. To ensure that the interactions with such texts lead to maximum student learning, teachers must provide significantly greater and more adroit instructional scaffolding—employing rereading, explanation, encouragement, and other supports within lessons. To accomplish this important shift successfully, teachers must have access to appropriate instructional resources and professional development that support them in providing such scaffolding.

Source: IRA, 2012

Preparing Students to Read Complex Text

PREPARING OUR STUDENTS TO READ COMPLEX TEXT involves our teaching them a variety of skills and strategies. This instruction should begin in the primary grades.

A number of literacy experts have offered ideas about what we can teach to support our students' engagement with complex text. For example, Shanahan et al. (2012) suggest that we strive to ensure that students experience success by focusing on building skills (e.g., decoding, fluency, vocabulary), establishing purposes for reading, and fostering motivation and persistence. These authors also recognize the importance of providing instructional resources and professional learning to support such instruction. Pearson and Hiebert (2012) suggest that teachers and students set purposes for reading, make connections to previously read text, and review and revisit themes.

In addition, we should teach students a variety of text structures and encourage them to understand the role of background knowledge in the reading process. As the focus of teaching moves from less complex text to more complex text, we should provide the scaffolds necessary to support this transition. Ideas might include Cross-Age Reading Experiences (McLaughlin, 2010), multiple ways of representing thinking, and student self-reflection.

As we contemplate various issues concerning text complexity, Hiebert (2012) recommends that we take seven actions right now to develop students' ability to read complex text:

1. Focus on knowledge.
2. Make connections between new and existing knowledge.
3. Activate students' passion for reading.
4. Develop vocabulary in narrative and informational texts.
5. Increase the volume of student reading.
6. Build students' reading stamina (i.e., ability to sustain attention).
7. Identify benchmark or "anchor" texts.

As we take these actions, we also need to provide students with extended opportunities for reading, writing, and discussion to ensure that they are prepared to read complex text. It is important to remember that when the Standards are implemented, students will be at different points in their learning. Some will be aware of text complexity and its related processes from the primary grades forward; others will be in middle school or high school when they begin to learn about reading complex text.

Instruction in how to approach reading a complex text can occur in a variety of instructional settings, but several factors should be considered before this instruction takes place. Key factors include motivation, multiple modes of representing thinking, reading comprehension strategies, vocabulary, and background knowledge. In addition, students need to be taught the concepts outlined in the ELA Standards—both the standards for the students' current grade level and those for lower grade levels, upon which the students' current grade-level standards are based. For example, scaffolding students' ability to read complex text may require instruction in essential reading skills, such as asking and answering questions, recognizing text structures, and citing textual evidence.

Pearson and Hiebert (2013) note that integrating complex text as an expectation of the Common Core will not result in students' reading it successfully. They suggest that students will need increased teacher scaffolding in multiple areas including the nature of text, language, and academic conversations.

In the Common Core Classroom

Jamal, Tracy, and Lisette are three middle school reading teachers. They teach sixth, seventh, and eighth grade, respectively, and have been working together to implement the CCSS as a subgroup of their school's implementation team. As they have studied and deconstructed the ELA Standards, one of their enduring focuses has been complex text. All three teachers are very familiar with the expectations of the Common Core concerning this topic, which, simply stated, note that every student will read complex text. In addition, all three are reading specialists, so they have an in-depth understanding not only of how to teach reading but also of how to integrate appropriate texts in their teaching. For example, these teachers meet periodically to determine anchor texts for their grade levels.

In the reflections that follow, each educator thinks through how to reconcile what he or she knows to be "best practice" in the teaching of reading with the expectations of the Common Core.

Jamal

I know that when I share more challenging text with our students, I typically find an alternative means of doing so. For example, I might share the text through teacher read-aloud or invite students to listen to it on CD. Of course, both of these options would be preceded by activating background knowledge and followed by in-depth discussion. Then, the Common Core State Standards were adopted by our state, and we found ourselves contemplating two new questions: (1) What exactly is complex text? (2) How can we teach our students to read complex text?

I learned exactly what complex text is by working with my school's CCSS implementation team. I knew it was challenging text. I knew the goal was to read it and gain insights through deep comprehension, but it took me a while—in fact, I am still dealing with this aspect of it—to understand how text complexity came to be included in the Common Core. I understand the need to ensure that students read more challenging text, but I am still struggling with ensuring that my students can read complex text as it is described in the Text Complexity: Qualitative Measures Rubrics for Literature and Informational Text. I am specifically concerned about expecting my students to read text that is described as *highly complex* and has language that is heavily "abstract," "generally abstract and archaic," and "purposefully misleading."

Tracy

We learned about complex text in materials provided by the Common Core. We particularly focused on CCSS Appendix A, which provided information about numerous aspects of text complexity. We attempted to reconcile the beliefs espoused by the Common Core with what we know about teaching more challenging texts. One particularly challenging aspect of this part of our deliberations was that the writers of the CCSS want our students to be college and career ready to read complex text. It seems as if they think that complex text will solve reading problems as they currently exist.

A high number of our middle school students struggle to comprehend text. We need to ensure that we do everything we can for our students, including activating background knowledge and teaching reading comprehension strategies.

Lisette

As we began thinking about how to teach our students to read complex text, we focused on what we knew to be best practices. We have, on average, about 30 students in our classrooms. We know they are reading at multiple levels, so we felt compelled to continue to scaffold student instruction of what we have labeled "increasingly complex text."

We have integrated multiple Common Core State Standards in our lessons to create rich instructional tasks. Our goal is to complete the year with students reading, what for them would be "complex text"—a goal they would reach by reading increasing complex text throughout the year. We also decided to continue to feature more complex text in our teacher read-alouds and provide a greater number of more complex texts on CD, so students could listen to them.

Further, we felt compelled to develop several activities to ensure our students believed they were active, successful readers. Ideas that are now part of our curriculums include the following:

- Teaching our students to engage in deep comprehension from a critical perspective—to read deeply, question the author and the text, and take action.

- Teaching our students to mark up and annotate text. [See Figures 4.6 and 4.7 for student examples of marked-up and annotated narrative and informational text, respectively.]

- Encouraging students to use multiple modes of representing their thinking—including sketching—to help increase their comprehension and promote deeper and more meaningful discussion.

- Encouraging students to participate in our school wide reading program, Ten Minutes More, in which every student reads engaging text for 10 minutes in addition to the time he or she had previously spent reading. Student interest and self-selection are key parts of this process, in which the whole school engages. The goal is to increase students' reading volume and stamina.

- Inviting students to maintain electronic Complex Text Journals, in which they add titles and short summaries to their "Staircases of Complex Text" to show progress throughout the academic year. When commenting on students' journals, we praise their progress—not only in text complexity but in volume and stamina, as well.

- Engaging students in Cross-Age Reading Experiences (CARE) that provide opportunities to experience success in reading when they partner with a high school student or a student in a lower grade level.

FIGURE 4.6 ● Marked-Up, Annotated Narrative Text for the Short Story "The Necklace"

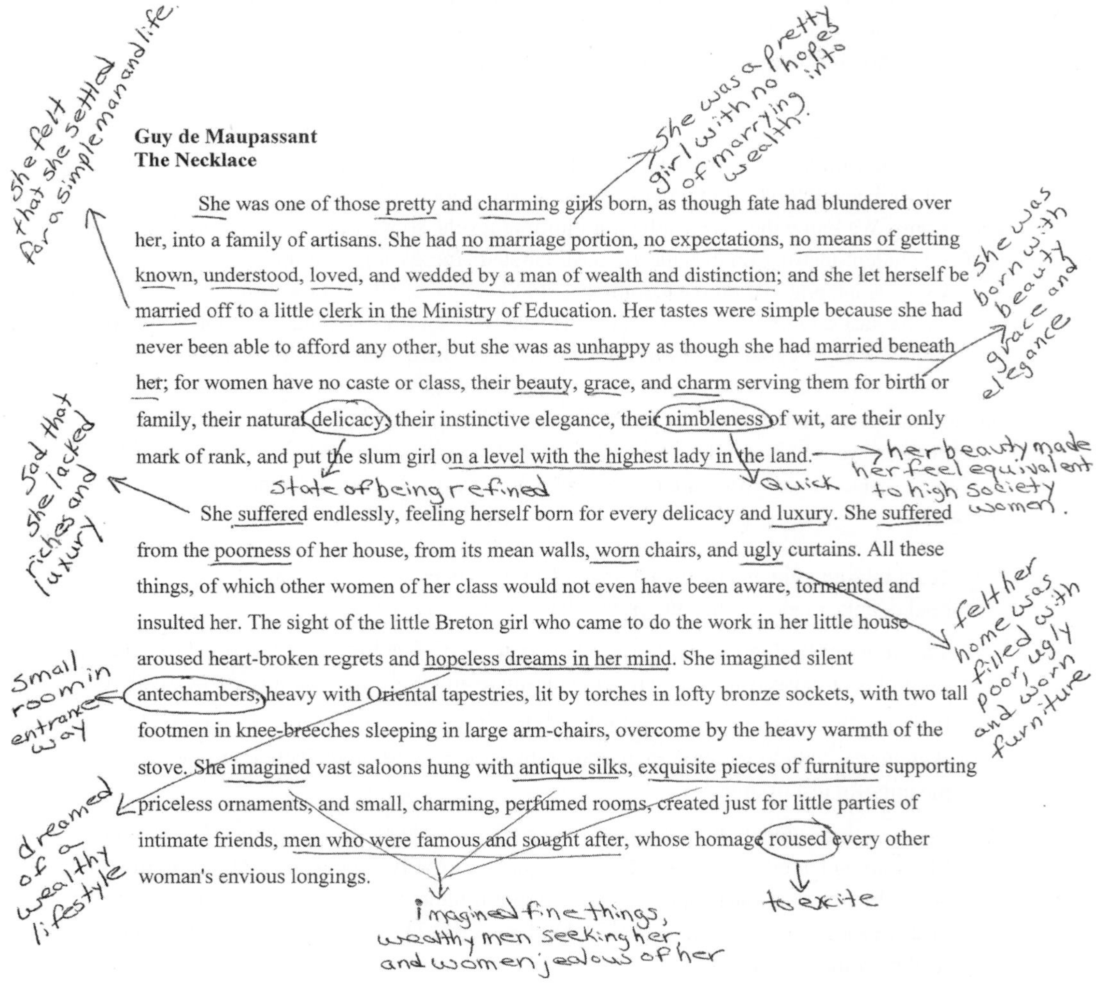

Guy de Maupassant
The Necklace

She was one of those pretty and charming girls born, as though fate had blundered over her, into a family of artisans. She had no marriage portion, no expectations, no means of getting known, understood, loved, and wedded by a man of wealth and distinction; and she let herself be married off to a little clerk in the Ministry of Education. Her tastes were simple because she had never been able to afford any other, but she was as unhappy as though she had married beneath her; for women have no caste or class, their beauty, grace, and charm serving them for birth or family, their natural delicacy, their instinctive elegance, their nimbleness of wit, are their only mark of rank, and put the slum girl on a level with the highest lady in the land.

She suffered endlessly, feeling herself born for every delicacy and luxury. She suffered from the poorness of her house, from its mean walls, worn chairs, and ugly curtains. All these things, of which other women of her class would not even have been aware, tormented and insulted her. The sight of the little Breton girl who came to do the work in her little house aroused heart-broken regrets and hopeless dreams in her mind. She imagined silent antechambers, heavy with Oriental tapestries, lit by torches in lofty bronze sockets, with two tall footmen in knee-breeches sleeping in large arm-chairs, overcome by the heavy warmth of the stove. She imagined vast saloons hung with antique silks, exquisite pieces of furniture supporting priceless ornaments, and small, charming, perfumed rooms, created just for little parties of intimate friends, men who were famous and sought after, whose homage roused every other woman's envious longings.

Handwritten annotations:
- she felt that she settled for a simple man and life
- She was a pretty girl with no hopes of marrying into wealth.
- she was born with beauty grace and elegance
- sad that she lacked riches and luxury
- state of being refined
- her beauty made her feel equivalent to high society women.
- Quick
- felt her home was filled with poor ugly and worn furniture
- small room in entrance way
- dreamed of a wealthy lifestyle
- imagined fine things, wealthy men seeking her and women jealous of her
- to excite

FIGURE 4.7 ● Marked-Up, Annotated Informational Text from a Textbook

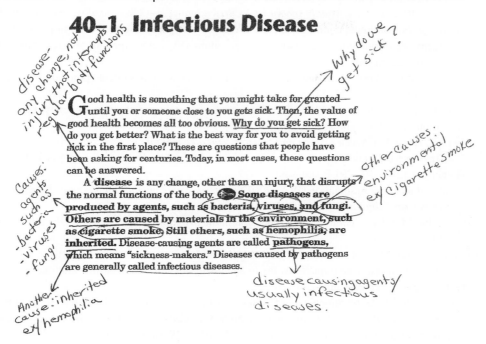

Teaching students in grades 6–8 to read increasingly complex text is essential. However, it is also important to remember that complex text is only one of the types of text with which students need to engage. Opportunities for students to read independent-level texts, which they can read on their own, and instructional-level texts, which they can read with some help from the teacher, are still essential for students to become college and career ready.

REFERENCES

American College Testing (ACT). (2006). *Reading between the lines: What the ACT reveals about college readiness in reading.* Iowa City, IA: Author.

Coleman, D., & Pimentel, S. (2012a). *Revised publishers' criteria for the Common Core State Standards in English language arts and literacy, grades K–2.* Washington, DC: National Governors Association Center for Best Practices & Council of Chief State School Officers. Retrieved from http://www.corestandards.org/assets/Publishers_Criteria_for_K-2.pdf.

Coleman, D., & Pimentel, S. (2012b). *Revised publishers' criteria for the Common Core State Standards in English language arts and literacy, grades 3–12.* Washington, DC: National

Governors Association Center for Best Practices & Council of Chief State School Officers. Retrieved from http://www.corestandards.org/assets/Publishers_Criteria_for_3-12.pdf

EngageNY. (2012, Dec. 5). *Middle school ELA curriculum video—Close reading of a text: MLK "Letter from Birmingham jail* [Video]. New York, NY: Author. Retrieved from http://www .engageny.org/resource/middle-school-ela-curriculum-video-close-reading-of-a-text-mlk-letter- from-birmingham-jail.

Gewertz, C. (2012, April 25). Common standards ignite debate over student "prereading" exercises. *Education Week,* pp. 1, 22–23.

Hiebert, E. F. (Dec. 2011/Jan. 2012). The Common Core's staircase of text complexity: Getting the size of the first step right. *Reading Today, 29*(3), 2–3.

Hiebert, E. H. (2012). *Seven actions that teachers can take right now: Text complexity.* Santa Cruz, CA: TextProject, University of California. Retrieved from http://textproject.org/assets/Uploads/ Hiebert_2012-03-10_CRLP-slides.pdf.

International Reading Association (IRA). (2012). *Literacy implementation guidance for the ELA Common Core Standards.* Newark, DE: Author.

McLaughlin, M. (2010). *Guided Comprehension in the primary grades.* Newark, DE: International Reading Association.

MetaMetrics. (2012). Text complexity grade bands and Lexile bands. *Lexile Framework for Reading.* Retrieved from http://www.lexile.com/using-lexile/lexile-measures-and-the-ccssi/ text-complexity-grade-bands-and-lexile-ranges/.

National Governors Association Center for Best Practices & Council of Chief State School Officers (NGA & CCSSO). (2010a). *Common Core State Standards: English language arts and literacy in history/social studies, science, and technical subjects.* Washington, DC: Authors. Retrieved from www.corestandards.org/assets/CCSSI_ELA%20Standards.pdf.

National Governors Association Center for Best Practices & Council of Chief State School Officers (NGA & CCSSO). (2010b). Appendix A: Research supporting key elements of the standards. *Common Core State Standards.* Washington, DC: Authors. Retrieved from www.corestandards .org/assets/CCSSI_ELA%20Standards.pdf.

National Governors Association Center for Best Practices & Council of Chief State School Officers (NGA & CCSSO). (2010c). Appendix B: Text exemplars and sample performance tasks. *Common Core State Standards.* Washington, DC: Authors. Retrieved from http://www .corestandards.org/assets/Appendix_B.pdf.

National Governors Association Center for Best Practices & Council of Chief State School Officers (NGA & CCSSO). (2010d). *Suggested considerations for reader and task.* Washington, DC: Authors. Retrieved from http://programs.ccsso.org/projects/common%20core%20resources/ documents/Reader%20and%20Task%20Considerations.pdf

Pearson, P. D., & Hiebert, E. H. (2013). Understanding the Common Core State Standards. In L. M. Morrow, T. Shanahan, & K. K. Wixson (Eds.), *Teaching with the Common Core Standards for English Language Arts, PreK–2.* New York, NY: Guilford Press.

Shanahan, T., Fisher, D., & Frey, N. (2012). The challenge of challenging text. *Educational Leadership, 69*(6), 58–62.

Student Achievement Partners. (2013). Close reading model lessons. *Achievethecore.org.* Retrieved from http://www.achievethecore.org/page/752/featured-lessons.

LITERATURE AND INFORMATIONAL TEXTS CITED

de Maupassant, G. (1907). The necklace. In B. Matthews (Ed.), *The short story.* New York, NY: American Book. (Original work published 1884) Retrieved from http://www.bartleby.com/195/20.html.

The immune system and disease. (Chapter 40, p. 1031) Retrieved from http://www.downtownmagnets.org/ourpages/auto/2011/6/12/56461450/Ch%2040-1%20Infectious%20Diseases.pdf

Speaking and Listening

WHEN WE THINK ABOUT OUR STUDENTS successfully meeting the Common Core State Standards (CCSS) for Speaking and Listening, we should understand that these standards are inextricably linked to all the strands in the English Language Arts (ELA) Standards. Consequently, when we align our teaching with the expectations of the Speaking and Listening Standards, we do so within rich literacy tasks, in which all of the language arts are integrated.

Our goal in this chapter is to situate the Common Core State Speaking and Listening Standards within the theory and practice involved in the teaching of the English language arts. Specifically, we will focus on what students need to know and be able to do in reading to successfully to meet the expectations outlined in the Speaking and Listening Standards.

Lisa F. Young/Fotolia

This chapter is organized into four sections. In the first section, we discuss what the CCSS have to say about speaking and listening. In the second section, we examine what we know about speaking and listening. Next, we explore classroom examples of teaching ideas that support speaking and listening, as they are addressed in the CCSS. Finally, we consider reflections from several classroom teachers as they make choices in teaching to the CCSS.

Speaking and Listening in the CCSS

THE COLLEGE AND CAREER READINESS (CCR) ANCHOR STANDARDS for Speaking and Listening are presented in Table 5.1; these standards serve as the foundation of the CCSS for grades 6–8. The CCSS for Speaking and Listening are featured in Table 5.2; these standards detail the expectations for students in grades 6–8.

Specifically, the CCSS state that students in grades 6–8 should participate in a range of collaborative discussions, including paired, small-group, and whole-class discussions (NGA & CCSSO, 2010). The CCSS also state that these students should be able to visually, quantitatively, and orally interpret messages produced in diverse media formats, as well as recognize the purposes behind these messages. Students are also expected to evaluate the soundness of arguments and present findings in a coherent and pertinent manner, using appropriate eye contact, volume, and pronunciation. Finally, the CCSS for Speaking and Listening state that students should be able to integrate multimedia to strengthen claims and add interest to presentations. Students are also expected to adapt their speech to a variety of contexts and tasks.

TABLE 5.1 ● *College and Career Readiness Anchor Standards for Speaking and Listening*

Comprehension and Collaboration

1. Prepare for and participate effectively in a range of conversations and collaborations with diverse partners, building on others' ideas and expressing their own clearly and persuasively.
2. Integrate and evaluate information presented in diverse media and formats, including visually, quantitatively, and orally.
3. Evaluate a speaker's point of view, reasoning, and use of evidence and rhetoric.

Presentation of Knowledge and Ideas

4. Present information, findings, and supporting evidence such that listeners can follow the line of reasoning and the organization, development, and style are appropriate to task, purpose, and audience.
5. Make strategic use of digital media and visual displays of data to express information and enhance understanding of presentations.
6. Adapt speech to a variety of contexts and communicative tasks, demonstrating command of formal English when indicated or appropriate.

TABLE 5.2 • *Common Core State Standards for Speaking and Listening, Grades 6–8*

Grade 6 Students:	Grade 7 Students:	Grade 8 Students:
Comprehension and Collaboration		
1. Engage effectively in a range of collaborative discussions (one-on-one, in groups, and teacher-led) with diverse partners on *grade 6 topics, texts, and issues*, building on others' ideas and expressing their own clearly.	1. Engage effectively in a range of collaborative discussions (one-on-one, in groups, and teacher-led) with diverse partners on *grade 7 topics, texts, and issues*, building on others' ideas and expressing their own clearly.	1. Engage effectively in a range of collaborative discussions (one-on-one, in groups, and teacher-led) with diverse partners on *grade 8 topics, texts, and issues*, building on others' ideas and expressing their own clearly.
a. Come to discussions prepared, having read or studied required material; explicitly draw on that preparation by referring to evidence on the topic, text, or issue to probe and reflect on ideas under discussion.	a. Come to discussions prepared, having read or researched material under study; explicitly draw on that preparation by referring to evidence on the topic, text, or issue to probe and reflect on ideas under discussion.	a. Come to discussions prepared, having read or researched material under study; explicitly draw on that preparation by referring to evidence on the topic, text, or issue to probe and reflect on ideas under discussion.
b. Follow rules for collegial discussions, set specific goals and deadlines, and define individual roles as needed.	b. Follow rules for collegial discussions, track progress toward specific goals and deadlines, and define individual roles as needed.	b. Follow rules for collegial discussions and decision-making, track progress toward specific goals and deadlines, and define individual roles as needed.
c. Pose and respond to specific questions with elaboration and detail by making comments that contribute to the topic, text, or issue under discussion.	c. Pose questions that elicit elaboration and respond to others' questions and comments with relevant observations and ideas that bring the discussion back on topic as needed.	c. Pose questions that connect the ideas of several speakers and respond to others' questions and comments with relevant evidence, observations, and ideas.
d. Review the key ideas expressed and demonstrate understanding of multiple perspectives through reflection and paraphrasing.	d. Acknowledge new information expressed by others and, when warranted, modify their own views.	d. Acknowledge new information expressed by others, and, when warranted, qualify or justify their own views in light of the evidence presented.

(continued)

TABLE 5.2 ● (continued)

2. Interpret information presented in diverse media and formats (e.g., visually, quantitatively, orally) and explain how it contributes to a topic, text, or issue under study.	2. Analyze the main ideas and supporting details presented in diverse media and formats (e.g., visually, quantitatively, orally) and explain how the ideas clarify a topic, text, or issue under study.	2. Analyze the purpose of information presented in diverse media and formats (e.g., visually, quantitatively, orally) and evaluate the motives (e.g., social, commercial, political) behind its presentation.
3. Delineate a speaker's argument and specific claims, distinguishing claims that are supported by reasons and evidence from claims that are not.	3. Delineate a speaker's argument and specific claims, evaluating the soundness of the reasoning and the relevance and sufficiency of the evidence.	3. Delineate a speaker's argument and specific claims, evaluating the soundness of the reasoning and relevance and sufficiency of the evidence and identifying when irrelevant evidence is introduced.

Presentation of Knowledge and Ideas

4. Present claims and findings, sequencing ideas logically and using pertinent descriptions, facts, and details to accentuate main ideas or themes; use appropriate eye contact, adequate volume, and clear pronunciation.	4. Present claims and findings, emphasizing salient points in a focused, coherent manner with pertinent descriptions, facts, details, and examples; use appropriate eye contact, adequate volume, and clear pronunciation.	4. Present claims and findings, emphasizing salient points in a focused, coherent manner with relevant evidence, sound valid reasoning, and well-chosen details; use appropriate eye contact, adequate volume, and clear pronunciation.
5. Include multimedia components (e.g., graphics, images, music, sound) and visual displays in presentations to clarify information.	5. Include multimedia components and visual displays in presentations to clarify claims and findings and emphasize salient points.	5. Integrate multimedia and visual displays into presentations to clarify information, strengthen claims and evidence, and add interest.
6. Adapt speech to a variety of contexts and tasks, demonstrating command of formal English when indicated or appropriate. (See grade 6 Language standards 1 and 3 on page 52 for specific expectations.)	6. Adapt speech to a variety of contexts and tasks, demonstrating command of formal English when indicated or appropriate. (See grade 7 Language standards 1 and 3 on page 52 for specific expectations.)	6. Adapt speech to a variety of contexts and tasks, demonstrating command of formal English when indicated or appropriate. (See grade 8 Language standards 1 and 3 on page 52 for specific expectations.)

What We Know about Teaching Speaking and Listening

AS JOHNSTON, IVEY, AND FAULKNER (2011) note in their article on classroom discussion, language is a powerful tool. As such, it can have a negative or positive influence on building students' relationships, developing their identities, and building their relationships with literacy. The CCSS embrace this concept, as well, by focusing on an integrated model of the English language arts.

Speaking and listening are both language processes. Speaking is an *expressive* process, in which we use oral language to communicate. Unlike writing, in speaking, much of what we express is not revised or edited. Listening is a *receptive* process, in which we take in information from other sources. Interestingly, students' listening comprehension is typically higher than their reading comprehension.

Discussion is the most prevalent way in which we engage students in speaking and listening in our classrooms. We encourage students to participate in discussions in multiple formats—whole class, small group, and pairs—and each format offers unique benefits. For example, participating in a whole-class discussion affords students the opportunity to exchange ideas with many peers. In contrast, participating in a small-group discussion provides students with opportunities to talk with only a few peers which is often viewed as a less challenging environment for students who struggle with sharing their ideas with a large group. Finally, talking in pairs provides students with a secure "turn and talk to your neighbor" environment. When scaffolding instruction, we can change from a whole-group to a small-group or paired discussion, engaging in the gradual release of responsibility.

Berne and Clark (2006) note that having literary discussions provides a way for students to create their own meanings, rather than being taught what the text represents. Gambrell (2004) concurs, noting that during collaborative discussions, students construct their own meanings and develop deeper understandings of a text. She further notes the changing nature of discussions, which are now viewed as peer-led, teacher-led, and computer-mediated discussions.

Research suggests that students need to be taught how to contribute to discussions and how to use comprehension strategies to think through a text (Berne & Clark, 2006). For example, to participate successfully in discussion groups or Literature Circles, students understand group behavior. This includes knowing that everyone in the group has worthwhile information to contribute and that no individual should dominate the discussion. Students also need to learn to be accepting, not critical, of others' ideas. Whether speaking or listening, students should keep the focus of the discussion on the contributions of all of the individuals involved.

Johnston et al. (2011) offer the following suggestions for guiding classroom discussion:

- Invite students to answer open-ended questions, and listen attentively as they respond.
- Encourage students to be aware of their own thinking processes.
- Encourage students to become independent, strategic readers and productive decision makers.
- Communicate using positive language to create a community of learners in the classroom.

Classroom talk is an important component of students' learning. When we cultivate it, we help students learn to problem solve and use strategies that may inspire others (Johnston et al., 2011). Gambrell (2004) notes that having small-group discussions helps develop positive student qualities, such as using higher-level thinking skills, being challenged to examine one's own thinking and challenging others' thinking, developing comprehension strategies, and being motivated.

Researchers concur that having classroom discussions has numerous benefits (Gambrell, 2004; Johnston et al., 2011; Ketch, 2005; Kucan & Beck, 2003). We need to promote discussions in our classrooms and provide students with the time and opportunities to engage in them.

Teaching Speaking and Listening in the Common Core Classroom

TO HELP OUR STUDENTS MEET THE CCSS for Speaking and Listening, we should make special efforts to infuse speaking and listening into our teaching. We can do this at multiple levels, ranging from everyday approaches, such as engaging in academic discussions and using books on CD, to teaching various fluency techniques and reading comprehension strategy applications, to encouraging students to self-select specific projects involving speaking and listening. We need to remember to be attentive to students' interest and motivation at all levels.

Oral Reading Fluency

We can teach students to use various ways to develop their oral reading fluency that offer opportunities to engage in speaking and listening. Reader's Theater and Cross-Age Reading Experiences are two examples of effective methods; these and other approaches are described in the following sections.

Reader's Theater   In Reader's Theatre, we should select texts that include dialogue; ready-to-use scripts are available online at a number of websites. We should invite students to read different roles to develop fluency skills.

Cross-Age Reading Experiences   Engaging in Cross-Age Reading Experiences provides students with multiple opportunities to enrich their oral reading fluency. For example, the upper-grade reader can be a good fluency model for the younger reader when the students engage in choral or echo reading. Together, the students can read along to a CD of the text or engage in Reader's Theater.

Paired Oral Reading   In Paired Oral Reading, students work with partners to develop oral reading fluency (Koskinen, Blum, Bisson, Phillips, Creamer, & Baker, 1999):

- Partners select passages and read them silently. Then each student reads his or her passage orally three times, while the other student raises questions and offers positive suggestions.
- Students sit side by side, holding the book between them. Together, they make predictions, decide who will begin reading, and ask one another for help as needed.

Oral Recitation Lesson   For this approach, select a text with dialogue and/or one that requires the use of simple props to act it out. Engage in the initial read-through of the text and model fluent oral reading for students. Select a strategy that will further develop students' understanding of the text—for instance, a summary, story map, or graphic organizer. Discuss the story and then focus on the prosodic elements, which include the rhythm, stress, and intonation of speech. Invite students to dramatize the text (Rasinski & Zutell, 1990).

Strategy Applications

Two strategy applications for developing students' skills in speaking and listening are Say Something and Save the Last Word for Me. Both of these strategy applications support the CCSS for Speaking and Listening.

Say Something   When engaging in Say Something, students work in pairs as they read a text, stopping at predetermined points (Short, Harste, & Burke, 1996) to say something about the text to his or her partner. Students may choose the stopping points or we can provide them; Subheadings make good stopping points in informational text. Figure 5.1 shows an example of Say Something in which student partners exchange comments during their reading of their biology textbook.

When students use Say Something, they make connections with the text during reading. This helps students to comprehend text through reading and discussion. The comprehension strategies addressed include monitoring and making connections.

Save the Last Word for Me   Save the Last Word for Me (Short et al., 1996) provides a structure that students can use to discuss the information in a text. It also helps students to

FIGURE 5.1 ● Say Something Using a Text about Diseases

Text: *Biology* (Miller & Levine, 2008, pp. 1031–1033)

Stopping Point 1

Student 1: "I didn't know that years ago, people thought diseases were caused by evil spirits and curses."

Student 2: "I know that diseases are caused by germs."

Stopping Point 2

Student 1: "Diseases can be carried by insects."

Student 2: "When a disease carrying insect bites a person, the person becomes infected with the disease."

Stopping Point 3

Student 1: "I didn't know that pathogens, which are infectious agents that cause disease, destroy cells as they grow."

Student 2: "I didn't know that bacteria release toxins that damage organisms."

Stopping Point 4

Student 1: "Viruses are small particles that attack and reproduce inside living cells."

Student 2: "The common cold and the flu are examples of diseases that are caused by viruses."

---

make connections to and evaluate the information presented. The comprehension strategies addressed include making connections and evaluating.

To begin, we introduce a text and invite students to read it. After reading, each student completes an index card with the following information:

- **Side 1:** The student writes a quote, idea, phrase, or fact that he or she thinks will evoke a response from readers. The student also provides the page and paragraph numbers, so he or she can easily access the information in context.
- **Side 2:** The student writes his or her reaction to the information recorded on side 1.

After completing their index cards, students discuss them within small groups. Each student shares the quote, idea, phrase, or fact recorded on side 1 of the card, and then each group member shares his or her thoughts about that information. The student who shared the information from his or her card is the last person to respond to it. Therefore, the sequence of the speakers supports the title Save the Last Word for Me. Figure 5.2 shows an example of a student's completed index card based on a text about the American Revolutionary War (Bobrick, 2004).

Projects

A variety of projects focus on oral language skills, including debates, Press Conference, Discussion Circles, and Transmediations. All of these projects meet the expectations of the CCSS for Speaking and Listening.

Debate   In a debate, a topic is selected for which students can have two different perspectives. Then, students present arguments for and against the topic. When students engage in a debate, they integrate speaking and listening with the skills involved in developing and presenting an argument. A topic is selected and arguments for and against are presented.

To begin, students choose a topic and work in pairs to discover and discuss arguments for and against it. They record their findings on the Discussion Web (Alvermann, 1991): a graphic organizer that provides a structure for thinking through the talking points.

FIGURE 5.2 ● Save the Last Word for Me Using a Text about the American Revolutionary War

Front

"We hold these truths to be self-evident, that all men are created equal, that they are endowed by their Creator with certain inalienable Rights, that among these are Life, Liberty, and the pursuit of Happiness. That to secure these rights, Governments are instituted among Men, deriving their just powers from the consent of the governed . . ." (p. 4)

Back

I chose this quote because it means a lot to me historically. It was because of the American Revolution that the Declaration of Independence was created. The thirteen colonies in North America wanted to become independent from Great Britain and had ideals of becoming a democratic government. If it wasn't for the American Revolutionary War, also called the War of Independence, we would not have freedom and equality today.

Source: Bobrick, B. (2004). *Fight for freedom: The American Revolutionary War*. New York: Atheneum Books for Young Readers.

The components of the Discussion Web include the topic, the pro and con arguments, a conclusion, and a rationale. Student pairs continue to engage in discussion as they think through the texts to arrive at a conclusion: whether they are for or against the topic. Then, the students write their conclusion and rationale on the organizer. After each pair reaches its conclusion, a whole-class discussion ensues. The final outcome is a conclusion—with appropriate reasoning—that has been determined by the class.

Figure 5.3 shows a completed Discussion Web about the topic of raising the driving age to 18. Students completed the web using information from an article in *Upfront, The*

FIGURE 5.3 ● Completed Discussion Web about the Driving Age

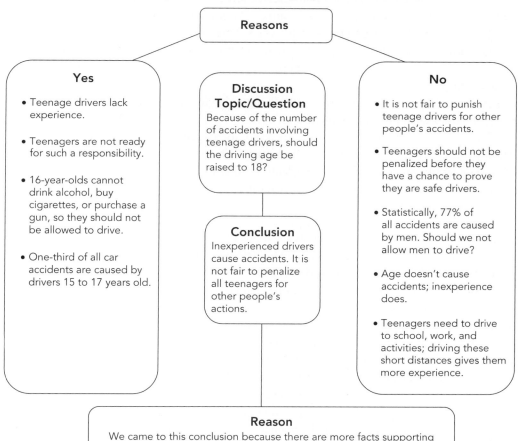

Debate topic: Should the driving age be raised to 18?

Reasons

Yes
- Teenage drivers lack experience.
- Teenagers are not ready for such a responsibility.
- 16-year-olds cannot drink alcohol, buy cigarettes, or purchase a gun, so they should not be allowed to drive.
- One-third of all car accidents are caused by drivers 15 to 17 years old.

Discussion Topic/Question
Because of the number of accidents involving teenage drivers, should the driving age be raised to 18?

Conclusion
Inexperienced drivers cause accidents. It is not fair to penalize all teenagers for other people's actions.

No
- It is not fair to punish teenage drivers for other people's accidents.
- Teenagers should not be penalized before they have a chance to prove they are safe drivers.
- Statistically, 77% of all accidents are caused by men. Should we not allow men to drive?
- Age doesn't cause accidents; inexperience does.
- Teenagers need to drive to school, work, and activities; driving these short distances gives them more experience.

Reason
We came to this conclusion because there are more facts supporting teenagers being allowed to drive at 16.

Newsmagazine For Teens ("Should the driving age," 2011), which is published by the *New York Times.*

Press Conference

Press Conference is an inquiry-based project that integrates reading, writing, speaking, and listening (McLaughlin, 2010). Students typically complete this inquiry-based project in disciplinary courses, such as science and social studies/history.

Students begin by self-selecting topics that are related to a current topic of study or a current event. Next, students reserve individual dates and times to present their Press Conferences and record the information on a class chart. (Because this project takes only a few minutes to present, scheduling one Press Conference per week works well.) Once the student has chosen a topic, he or she creates three research questions about the topic and responds to each using at least two sources. After completing the research, the student presents his or her Press Conference to the class. This includes sharing the information learned through research and responding to questions from students in the class. On occasion, the presenter will need to do further research to respond to a question from a class member.

The graphic organizer Questions into Paragraphs (McLaughlin, 1987), also known as QuIP, provides an appropriate structure for organizing a Press Conference. To complete the QuIP organizer, the student records his or her topic, generates three research questions about it, and answers to each question from two different sources. After completing the organizer, the student writes a paragraph summarizing the information presented. Figure 5.4 shows a completed QuIP organizer that served as the basis for a Press Conference on tsunamis.

Discussion Circles   Discussion Circles are designed to promote conversations about informational texts (McLaughlin, 2010). Students typically select a text from several we provide. Then, they read a designated segment of the text and engage in a small-group discussion. As students discuss the text, they can take on roles similar to those in Literature Circles: discussion leader, memorable passage finder, connector, illustrator, summarizer, and word finder. Students continue to read and discuss designated portions of the text until they have read all of it. After the final discussion, students may create extension projects to share their texts and thoughts with the class. Examples of projects include Press Conference, posters, and form poems (e.g., acrostics, definition poems).

Figures 5.5, 5.6, and 5.7 show materials used in Discussion Circles projects. Figure 5.5 is a Discussion Circle Planner: a graphic organizer on which students record questions, vocabulary, opinions, and evidence about the text. Figure 5.6 shows role-based ideas from a Discussion Circle about healthy school lunches; Students had read two texts about this topic ("Kids and food," 2012; Wood, 2012). Finally, Figure 5.7 shows an illustration created by the student who had the role of illustrator in the Discussion Circle.

FIGURE 5.4 ● Completed QuIP Graphic Organizer for Use in Press Conference Project

	Source A:	Source B:
	CBC News http://www.cbc.ca/news/world/story/2011/03/11/japanquake-tsunami.html	National Geographic http://news.nationalgeographic.com/news/2011/03/110311-tsunami-facts-japan-earthquake-hawaii/
1. What causes tsunamis?	Powerful earthquakes produce tsunamis.	Tsunamis are caused by underwater earthquakes, volcanic eruptions, or landslides.
2. How are communities affected by tsunamis?	Tsunamis can devastate communities by knocking down power lines, and by washing cars, homes, land and debris out to sea. Tsunamis can take the lives of thousands of people.	Tsunamis can kill thousands of people and people can be sucked under by waves. Flooding can move cars and demolish houses and beaches can be stripped away.
3. In what ways can people protect themselves from tsunamis?	People can listen for tsunami warnings. They can also get away from coastlines, move to higher ground, and move to higher floors if they are in a building.	For protection from tsunamis, people can listen to tsunami warnings, have an evacuation plan in place to move to a higher ground and never stay by the shore.

QuIP Summary:

Tsunamis are caused by underwater earthquakes, volcanic eruptions, or landslides. Tsunamis can kill thousands of people and devastate communities. They knock down power lines and wash homes, cars, and people out to sea. Tsunamis can also strip beaches. To protect themselves from tsunamis, people should listen for warning signals and have an evacuation plan. They can move away from coastlines and move to higher ground.

Transmediations   When students engage in Transmediations (McLaughlin, 2010), they transform information from one medium to another. In this project, the information already exists, but students focus on how to present that information in a new medium. For example, Figure 5.8 features a student-authored definition poem based on an informational text. The student transmediated several pages of the book *Oceanwatch* (Bramwell, 2001) by writing a poem defining coral reefs.

FIGURE 5.5 ● Discussion Circle Planner

	My Questions		Vocabulary to Discuss
	1.		1.
	2.		2.
	3.		3.

Text:

	My Opinions		Text–Based Evidence
	1.		1.
	2		2.
	3.		3.

FIGURE 5.6 ● Examples of Roles in Discussion Circles about Healthy School Lunches

Discussion Director:

1. What is your opinion on having more fruits and vegetables added to school lunches?
2. Should students be allowed more choices when going through the lunch line?
3. What do you suppose will happen when the new regulations are passed and the school lunch program provides healthier choices?

Memorable Passages:

Page 1
It is about improving school meals for children in school.

(continued)

FIGURE 5.6 ● *(continued)*

Page 2
It is about how the school lunch program has not been fixed for more than 15 years.

Page 2
It is about how 17 percent of the United States' children and teens are obese.

Connector:

Text-Self Connection
I try to eat healthier but when fatty foods are available, I chose the fatty foods. Therefore, I think healthier choices would be better in schools.

Text-Text Connection
This reminded me of an article I read presenting 10 tips for children to eat healthier.

Text-World Connection
Eating healthy is an issue that everyone needs to be concerned about, not just children.

Word Finder :

Word: overhaul	Page: 2	Paragraph: 1	Definition: to repair
Word: obese	Page: 2	Paragraph: 6	Definition: very fat or overweight
Word: implemented	Page: 3	Paragraph: 1	Definition: to carry out

Source: U.S. News
http://usnews.nbcnews.com/_news/2012/01/25/10234671-students-to-see-healthier-school-lunches-under-new-usdarules?lite
Additional source for Text-Text Connection:
http://kidshealth.org/parent/nutrition_center/healthy_eating/eating_tips.html

---

FIGURE 5.7 ● Illustration by Student Playing the Role of Illustrator in Discussion Circle

Illustrator:

I drew an apple because it makes me think about having more fruits and vegetables in school lunches.

FIGURE 5.8 ● Transmediation of an Informational Text into a Definition Poem about Coral Reefs

Text: *Oceanwatch* (Bramwell, 2001)

What is a coral reef?

Contains swarms of life

A complete ecosystem

Built from miniature animal skeletons

Contains thousands of species

Threatened by pollution and overharvesting

Sold to tourists

Fragile structure

That is a coral reef!

In the Common Core Classroom

Nikki, Jose, and Paul are eighth-grade middle school teachers who teach science, social studies, and English, respectively. They have been working together with a larger professional learning community to implement the Common Core in their district. After contemplating how to infuse more speaking and listening into their teaching, they decided to develop a project in which students would write form poems. When discussing this project, the teachers noted that it was important for students to feel comfortable speaking to the class and that students should be able to share something they felt was motivational.

These characteristics seemed to have been missing from the oral presentations Nikki, Jose, and Paul had done when they were in middle school. Nikki and Jose both reflected on their middle school experiences with speaking and listening:

Nikki

When I was in middle school, I dreaded any kind of oral presentation. Pretty much everything we were asked to present needed to be memorized, and often everyone in the class was required to research and memorize the same thing: a historical document, a scientific biography, or a less-than-interesting poem. I had 40 students in my eighth-grade class. I cannot begin to tell you how inept I felt as a speaker, but I can tell you that after listening to 39 other students deliver their memorized sections of a historical document, I vowed that I would never engage my students in such a boring activity.

Jose

My experiences were very similar. That is why we want to make sure that the speaking and listening tasks in which our students engage are meaningful, motivational, and unique.

Jose and Paul also commented on the success of the form-poem project they used with their students:

Jose

Our students really enjoyed creating form poems, especially diamantes. After writing the poems, the students shared and discussed them with partners and then with small groups. Finally, after receiving feedback in those settings, volunteers shared with the whole class. They explained why they had chosen the topic and format. Then they read the poem and responded to questions from the class.

Paul

It was clear that our students had not only taken ownership of their writing, but they also felt very comfortable sharing their poems orally and engaging in discussions about them.

Figure 5.9 features two student-authored diamantes, which are diamond-shaped form poems. Students presented their poems in a variety of formats, including digital media.

FIGURE 5.9 ● Student-Authored Diamantes

Union	Sun
Blue Industrious	Gigantic Inferno
Defending Freeing Struggling	Glowing Burning Illuminating
North Wealth Distress South	Incandescent Hot Opalescent Cold
Rebelling Denying Suffering	Rotating Spinning Revolving
Gray Agricultural	Luminous Opaque
Confederacy	Moon

During their planning of the form-poem project, the teachers integrated the following:

- Reading Literature Standard 10
- Reading Informational Text Standards 7 and 10
- Writing Standards 4, 6, and 10
- Speaking and Listening Standards 1, 5, and 6
- Language Standards 1, 2, 3, and 6

Integrating speaking and listening in our teaching is essential. Doing so will not only help our students to meet the expectations of the CCSS, but it will also help them to develop the skills that will ensure they are college and career ready.

REFERENCES

Alvermann, D. (1991). The discussion web: A graphic aid for learning across the curriculum. *The Reading Teacher, 45,* 92–99.

Berne, J. I., & Clark, K. F. (2006). Comprehension strategy use during peer-led discussions of text: Ninth graders tackle "The Lottery." *Journal of Adolescent and Adult Literacy, 49*(8), 674–686.

Gambrell, L. B. (2004). Shifts in the conversation: Teacher-led, peer-led, and computer-mediated discussions. *The Reading Teacher, 58*(2), 212–215.

Johnston, P. H., Ivey, G., & Faulkner, A. (2011). Talking in class: Remembering what is important about classroom talk. *The Reading Teacher, 65*(4), 232–237.

Ketch, A. (2005). Conversation: The comprehension connection. *The Reading Teacher, 59*(1), 8–13.

Koskinen, P., Blum, I., Bisson, S., Phillips, S., Creamer, T., & Baker, T. (1999). Shared reading, books, and audiotapes: Supporting diverse students in school and at home. *The Reading Teacher, 52*(5), 430–444.

Kucan, L., & Beck, I. L. (2003). Inviting students to talk about expository texts: A comparison of two discourse environments and their effects on comprehension. *Reading Research and Instruction, 42,* 1–29.

McLaughlin, E. M. (1987). QuIP: A writing strategy to improve comprehension of expository structure. *The Reading Teacher, 40*(7), 650–654.

McLaughlin, M. (2010). *Content area reading: Teaching and learning in an age of multiple literacies.* Boston, MA: Allyn & Bacon.

National Governors Association Center for Best Practices & Council of Chief State School Officers (NGA & CCSSO). (2010). *Common Core State Standards: English language arts and literacy in history/social studies, science, and technical subjects.* Washington, DC: Authors. Retrieved from www.corestandards.org/assets/CCSSI_ELA%20Standards.pdf.

Rasinski, T. V. & Zutell, J. B. (1990). Making a place for fluency instruction in the regular reading curriculum. *Reading Research and Instruction, 29*(2), 85–91.

Short, K. G., Harste, J. C., & Burke, C. (1996). *Creating classrooms for authors and inquirers.* Portsmouth, NH: Heinemann.

INFORMATIONAL TEXTS CITED

Bobrick, B. (2004). *Fight for freedom: The American Revolutionary War.* New York, NY: Atheneum Books.

Bramwell, M. (2001). *Oceanwatch.* DK Protecting Our Planet Series. New York, NY: Dorling Kindersley.

Kids and food: 10 tips for parents. (2012, Feb.). *KidsHealth.org.* Retrieved from http://kidshealth.org/parent/nutrition_center/healthy_eating/eating_tips.html.

Miller, K. R., & Levine, J. S. (2008). *Biology.* Upper Saddle River, NJ: Prentice-Hall.

Should the driving age be raised to 18? (2011, May 9). *Upfront, The Newsmagazine For Teens, New York Times.* Retrieved from http://teacher.scholastic.com/scholasticnews/indepth/upfront/debate/index.asp?article=d0508.

Wood, S. (2012, Jan. 25). Students to see healthier school lunches under new USDA rules. *U.S. News, NBC News.com.* Retrieved from http://usnews.nbcnews.com/_news/2012/01/25/10234671-students-to-see-healthier-school-lunches-under-new-usda-rules?lite.

chapter 6

Writing

TO TEACH OUR STUDENTS TO SUCCESSFULLY MEET the expectations of the Common Core State Writing Standards, we need to remember that the CCSS are based on an integrated language arts model. This is clearly reflected in the interaction among reading, writing, speaking and listening, and language in the Standards. The integrated language arts should also be evident in the rich instructional tasks we design in our standards-based lessons.

In this chapter, our goal is to situate the Common Core State Standards within the theory and practice involved in the teaching of writing. To accomplish this, we will examine what students need to know and be able to do to become proficient writers and successfully meet the expectations of the Common Core.

Annie Pickert Fuller/Pearson

This chapter is divided into four sections. First, we delineate the Common Core expectations for Writing. Then, we examine what is currently viewed as best practice in the teaching of writing. Next, we explore a range of teaching ideas that support writing as it is addressed in the CCSS. Finally, we consider a vignette of one classroom teacher's choices for teaching to the Common Core.

The CCSS Writing Standards

THE CCSS FOR WRITING ARE UNIQUE IN TERMS of the expectations they set for students. The content addressed in the standards ranges from the writing process, to specific types of language (e.g., figurative language), to narrative and informational writing, and specific types of writing, such as persuasion and argument and research/inquiry (NGA & CCSSO, 2010a). The CCSS also address writing for short and long durations.

The College and Career Readiness (CCR) Anchor Standards for Writing delineate what students should know and be able to do by the end of each grade. As shown in Table 6.1, the CCR Standards are organized according into four clusters, or categories (NGA & CCSSO, 2010a):

1. Text Types and Purposes
2. Production and Distribution of Writing
3. Research to Build and Present Knowledge
4. Range of Writing

These standards also serve as the foundation of the CCSS for Writing, which delineate the writing skills and knowledge that students in grades 6–8 should be able to do by the end of each grade level. As shown in Table 6.2, the CCSS for Writing are organized into the same four clusters as the College and Career Readiness Anchor Standards (NGA & CCSSO, 2010a).

The Writing Standards are wide ranging and include student expectations in aspects of writing from coherence and organization to argument in a number of areas. For example, in the cluster Text Types and Purposes, expectations focus on writing arguments (Standard 1), informational/explanatory texts (Standard 2), and narratives (Standard 3). It is interesting to note that in terms of general expectations, the standards are the same for students across grades 6, 7, and 8. Examples of student writing that meet the CCSS criteria for particular types of writing at different grade levels are provided in Appendix C of the CCSS (NGA & CCSSO, 2010b).

In the cluster Production and Distribution of Writing, student expectations address qualities of writing, such as clarity, coherence, organization, and style (Standard 4); following the writing process with varying degrees of scaffolding (Standard 5); and using technology to produce and publish writing (Standard 5). Once again, the standards are

TABLE 6.1 ● *College and Career Readiness Anchor Standards for Writing*

Text Types and Purposes*

1. Write arguments to support claims in an analysis of substantive topics or texts, using valid reasoning and relevant and sufficient evidence.

2. Write informative/explanatory texts to examine and convey complex ideas and information clearly and accurately through the effective selection, organization, and analysis of content.

3. Write narratives to develop real or imagined experiences or events using effective technique, well-chosen details, and well-structured event sequences.

Production and Distribution of Writing

4. Produce clear and coherent writing in which the development, organization, and style are appropriate to task, purpose, and audience.

5. Develop and strengthen writing as needed by planning, revising, editing, rewriting, or trying a new approach.

6. Use technology, including the Internet, to produce and publish writing and to interact and collaborate with others.

Research to Build and Present Knowledge

7. Conduct short as well as more sustained research projects based on focused questions, demonstrating understanding of the subject under investigation.

8. Gather relevant information from multiple print and digital sources, assess the credibility and accuracy of each source, and integrate the information while avoiding plagiarism.

9. Draw evidence from literary or informational texts to support analysis, reflection, and research.

Range of Writing

10. Write routinely over extended time frames (time for research, reflection, and revision) and shorter time frames (a single sitting or a day or two) for a range of tasks, purposes, and audiences.

---

*These broad types of writing include many subgenres. See Appendix A for definitions of key writing types.

essentially the same across grade levels but build in terms of specific expectations from grade to grade.

The third cluster in the CCSS Writing standards is Research to Build and Present Knowledge. In this cluster, student expectations focus on conducting short research

TABLE 6.2 • *Common Core State Standards for Writing, Grades 6–8*

Grade 6 Students:	Grade 7 Students:	Grade 8 Students:
Text Types and Purposes		
1. Write arguments to support claims with clear reasons and relevant evidence.	1. Write arguments to support claims with clear reasons and relevant evidence.	1. Write arguments to support claims with clear reasons and relevant evidence.
a. Introduce claim(s) and organize the reasons and evidence clearly.	a. Introduce claim(s), acknowledge alternate or opposing claims, and organize the reasons and evidence logically.	a. Introduce claim(s), acknowledge and distinguish the claim(s) from alternate or opposing claims, and organize the reasons and evidence logically.
b. Support claim(s) with clear reasons and relevant evidence, using credible sources and demonstrating an understanding of the topic or text.	b. Support claim(s) with logical reasoning and relevant evidence, using accurate, credible sources and demonstrating an understanding of the topic or text.	b. Support claim(s) with logical reasoning and relevant evidence, using accurate, credible sources and demonstrating an understanding of the topic or text.
c. Use words, phrases, and clauses to clarify the relationships among claim(s) and reasons.	c. Use words, phrases, and clauses to create cohesion and clarify the relationships among claim(s), reasons, and evidence.	c. Use words, phrases, and clauses to create cohesion and clarify the relationships among claim(s), counterclaims, reasons, and evidence.
d. Establish and maintain a formal style.	d. Establish and maintain a formal style.	d. Establish and maintain a formal style.
e. Provide a concluding statement or section that follows from the argument presented.	e. Provide a concluding statement or section that follows from and supports the argument presented.	e. Provide a concluding statement or section that follows from and supports the argument presented.

(continued)

TABLE 6.2 ● (continued)

Text Types and Purposes (continued)

2. Write informative/explanatory texts to examine a topic and convey ideas, concepts, and information through the selection, organization, and analysis of relevant content.

  a. Introduce a topic; organize ideas, concepts, and information, using strategies such as definition, classification, comparison/contrast, and cause/effect; include formatting (e.g., headings), graphics (e.g., charts, tables), and multimedia when useful to aiding comprehension.

  b. Develop the topic with relevant facts, definitions, concrete details, quotations, or other information and examples.

  c. Use appropriate transitions to clarify the relationships among ideas and concepts.

  d. Use precise language and domain-specific vocabulary to inform about or explain the topic.

  e. Establish and maintain a formal style.

  f. Provide a concluding statement or section that follows from the information or explanation presented.

2. Write informative/explanatory texts to examine a topic and convey ideas, concepts, and information through the selection, organization, and analysis of relevant content.

  a. Introduce a topic clearly, previewing what is to follow; organize ideas, concepts, and information, using strategies such as definition, classification, comparison/contrast, and cause/effect; include formatting (e.g., headings), graphics (e.g., charts, tables), and multimedia when useful to aiding comprehension.

  b. Develop the topic with relevant facts, definitions, concrete details, quotations, or other information and examples.

  c. Use appropriate transitions to create cohesion and clarify the relationships among ideas and concepts.

  d. Use precise language and domain-specific vocabulary to inform about or explain the topic.

  e. Establish and maintain a formal style.

  f. Provide a concluding statement or section that follows from the information or explanation presented.

2. Write informative/explanatory texts to examine a topic and convey ideas, concepts, and information through the selection, organization, and analysis of relevant content.

  a. Introduce a topic clearly, previewing what is to follow; organize ideas, concepts, and information into broader categories; include formatting (e.g., headings), graphics (e.g., charts, tables), and multimedia when useful to aiding comprehension.

  b. Develop the topic with relevant, well-chosen facts, definitions, concrete details, quotations, or other information and examples.

  c. Use appropriate and varied transitions to create cohesion and clarify the relationships among ideas and concepts.

  d. Use precise language and domain-specific vocabulary to inform about or explain the topic.

  e. Establish and maintain a formal style.

  f. Provide a concluding statement or section that follows from and supports the information or explanation presented.

(continued)

TABLE 6.2 • (continued)

3. Write narratives to develop real or imagined experiences or events using effective technique, relevant descriptive details, and well-structured event sequences.

a. Engage and orient the reader by establishing a context and introducing a narrator and/or characters; organize an event sequence that unfolds naturally and logically.

b. Use narrative techniques, such as dialogue, pacing, and description, to develop experiences, events, and/or characters.

c. Use a variety of transition words, phrases, and clauses to convey sequence and signal shifts from one time frame or setting to another.

d. Use precise words and phrases, relevant descriptive details, and sensory language to convey experiences and events.

e. Provide a conclusion that follows from the narrated experiences or events.

3. Write narratives to develop real or imagined experiences or events using effective technique, relevant descriptive details, and well-structured event sequences.

a. Engage and orient the reader by establishing a context and point of view and introducing a narrator and/or characters; organize an event sequence that unfolds naturally and logically.

b. Use narrative techniques, such as dialogue, pacing, description, and reflection, to develop experiences, events, and/or characters.

c. Use a variety of transition words, phrases, and clauses to convey sequence and signal shifts from one time frame or setting to another.

d. Use precise words and phrases, relevant descriptive details, and sensory language to capture the action and convey experiences and events.

e. Provide a conclusion that follows from the narrated experiences or events.

3. Write narratives to develop real or imagined experiences or events using effective technique, relevant descriptive details, and well-structured event sequences.

a. Engage and orient the reader by establishing a context and point of view and introducing a narrator and/or characters; organize an event sequence that unfolds naturally and logically.

b. Use narrative techniques, such as dialogue, pacing, description, and reflection, to develop experiences, events, and/or characters.

c. Use a variety of transition words, phrases, and clauses to convey sequence, signal shifts from one time frame or setting to another, and show the relationships among experiences and events.

d. Use precise words and phrases, relevant descriptive details, and sensory language to capture the action and convey experiences and events.

e. Provide a conclusion that follows from and reflects on the narrated experiences or events.

(continued)

TABLE 6.2 ● (continued)

Production and Distribution of Writing

4. Produce clear and coherent writing in which the development, organization, and style are appropriate to task, purpose, and audience. (Grade-specific expectations for writing types are defined in standards 1–3 above.)	4. Produce clear and coherent writing in which the development, organization, and style are appropriate to task, purpose, and audience. (Grade-specific expectations for writing types are defined in standards 1–3 above.)	4. Produce clear and coherent writing in which the development, organization, and style are appropriate to task, purpose, and audience. (Grade-specific expectations for writing types are defined in standards 1–3 above.)
5. With some guidance and support from peers and adults, develop and strengthen writing as needed by planning, revising, editing, rewriting, or trying a new approach. (Editing for conventions should demonstrate command of Language standards 1–3 up to and including grade 6 on page 53.)	5. With some guidance and support from peers and adults, develop and strengthen writing as needed by planning, revising, editing, rewriting, or trying a new approach, focusing on how well purpose and audience have been addressed. (Editing for Language standards 1–3 up to and including grade 7 on page 53.)	5. With some guidance and support from peers and adults, develop and strengthen writing as needed by planning, revising, editing, rewriting, or trying a new approach, focusing on how well purpose and audience have been addressed. (Editing for conventions should demonstrate command of Language standards 1–3 up to and including grade 8 on page 53.)
6. Use technology, including the Internet, to produce and publish writing as well as to interact and collaborate with others; demonstrate sufficient command of keyboarding skills to type a minimum of three pages in a single sitting.	6. Use technology, including the Internet, to produce and publish writing and link to and cite sources as well as to interact and collaborate with others, including linking to and citing sources.	6. Use technology, including the Internet, to produce and publish writing and present the relationships between information and ideas efficiently as well as to interact and collaborate with others.

(continued)

TABLE 6.2 • (continued)

Research to Build and Present Knowledge

7. Conduct short research projects to answer a question, drawing on several sources and refocusing the inquiry when appropriate.	7. Conduct short research projects to answer a question, drawing on several sources and generating additional related, focused questions for further research and investigation.	7. Conduct short research projects to answer a question (including a self-generated question), drawing on several sources and generating additional related, focused questions that allow for multiple avenues of exploration.
8. Gather relevant information from multiple print and digital sources; assess the credibility of each source; and quote or paraphrase the data and conclusions of others while avoiding plagiarism and providing basic bibliographic information for sources.	8. Gather relevant information from multiple print and digital sources, using search terms effectively; assess the credibility and accuracy of each source; and quote or paraphrase the data and conclusions of others while avoiding plagiarism and following a standard format for citation.	8. Gather relevant information from multiple print and digital sources, using search terms effectively; assess the credibility and accuracy of each source; and quote or paraphrase the data and conclusions of others while avoiding plagiarism and following a standard format for citation.
9. Draw evidence from literary or informational texts to support analysis, reflection, and research.	9. Draw evidence from literary or informational texts to support analysis, reflection, and research.	9. Draw evidence from literary or informational texts to support analysis, reflection, and research.
a. Apply *grade 6 Reading standards* to literature (e.g., "Compare and contrast texts in different forms or genres [e.g., stories and poems; historical novels and fantasy stories] in terms of their approaches to similar themes and topics").	a. Apply *grade 7 Reading standards* to literature (e.g., "Compare and contrast a fictional portrayal of a time, place, or character and a historical account of the same period as a means of understanding how authors of fiction use or alter history").	a. Apply *grade 8 Reading standards* to literature (e.g., "Analyze how a modern work of fiction draws on themes, patterns of events, or character types from myths, traditional stories, or religious works such as the Bible, including describing how the material is rendered new").

(continued)

TABLE 6.2 ● *(continued)*

Research to Build and Present Knowledge (continued)

b. Apply *grade 6 Reading standards* to literary nonfiction (e.g., "Trace and evaluate the argument and specific claims in a text, distinguishing claims that are supported by reasons and evidence from claims that are not").	b. Apply *grade 7 Reading standards* to literary nonfiction (e.g. "Trace and evaluate the argument and specific claims in a text, assessing whether the reasoning is sound and the evidence is relevant and sufficient to support the claims").	b. Apply *grade 8 Reading standards* to literary nonfiction (e.g., "Delineate and evaluate the argument and specific claims in a text, assessing whether the reasoning is sound and the evidence is relevant and sufficient; recognize when irrelevant evidence is introduced").

Range of Writing

10. Write routinely over extended time frames (time for research, reflection, and revision) and shorter time frames (a single sitting or a day or two) for a range of discipline-specific tasks, purposes, and audiences.	10. Write routinely over extended time frames (time for research, reflection, and revision) and shorter time frames (a single sitting or a day or two) for a range of discipline-specific tasks, purposes, and audiences.	10. Write routinely over extended time frames (time for research, reflection, and revision) and shorter time frames (a single sitting or a day or two) for a range of discipline-specific tasks, purposes, and audiences.

projects (Standard 7); gathering, evaluating, and citing information from multiple sources (Standard 8); and using evidence to support analysis, reflection, and research (Standard 9). Within this cluster, in particular, expectations of students clearly build across grades 6–8, especially within standard 9.

The final cluster, Range of Writing, includes only Standard 10. Student expectations focus on writing routinely for different durations (short versus long) and on writing for various discipline-specific tasks, purposes, and audiences.

What We Know about Teaching Writing

WRITING IS AN EXPRESSIVE THINKING PROCESS THAT PROVIDES us with opportunities to develop, communicate, and revise our messages. From this perspective, writing is clearly different from speaking, in which we may say something and later wish we had taken the time to think through and refine our message. Opportunities for reflection and revision are directly connected to our teaching writing from a revisionist perspective.

Research-Based Practices

Since 2007, two important documents about writing have been published by the Carnegie Foundation: *Writing Next: Effective Strategies to Improve Writing of Adolescents in Middle and High Schools* (Graham & Perin, 2007) and *Writing to Read*: *Evidence for How Writing Can Improve Reading* (Graham & Hebert, 2010). According to Graham and Perin, authors of *Writing Next*:

> Writing well is not just an option for young people—it is a necessity. Along with reading comprehension, writing skill is a predictor of academic success and a basic requirement for participation in civic life and in the global economy. (p. 3)

The message is clear: Writing is a life skill.

In their report, Graham and Perin (2007) suggest 11 elements of writing instruction found to be effective not only for developing the writing skills of adolescents but also for helping them "use writing as a tool for learning" (p. 4). Although these practices do not constitute a full writing curriculum, they provide both research-based and motivational strategies for teaching writing. The elements of effective instruction are as follows:

1. writing strategies—namely, planning, revising, and editing
2. summarizing
3. collaborative writing
4. setting specific but reasonable product goals
5. using computers
6. combining sentences

7. prewriting to generate and organize ideas

8. inquiry activities to analyze information and develop ideas and content

9. following a process approach

10. studying models of good writing

11. writing in the content areas

In the second report, *Writing to Read* (2010), authors Graham and Hebert align writing ability with students' ability to read text. The authors recommend three writing practices that enhance students' reading. The practices are listed here in order of the strength of their supporting research base:

1. **Encourage students to write about the texts they read.** Students' comprehension of content area texts improves when they write about what they read in these specific ways:

   ● by responding with a personal reaction to or analysis or interpretation of a text

   ● by writing a summary of a text

   ● by writing notes about a text

   ● by answering questions about a text or by creating and answering questions about a text

2. **Teach students the writing skills and processes necessary for creating a text.** Learning these skills and processes improves students' reading skills and comprehension. Specific topics for instruction include the following:

   ● the writing process, text structures, and paragraph- and sentence-writing skill (improves reading comprehension)

   ● spelling and sentence construction skills (improves reading fluency)

   ● spelling skills (improves word-reading skills)

3. **Increase the volume of student writing.** Students' reading comprehension improves when they produce their own texts on a more frequent basis (p. 13).

Using Technology in Writing

To encourage our students to meet the CCSS, we not only need to be good writing models who believe in the writing process, but we also need to focus on integrating technology in our writing. Infusing technology is another aspect of writing that can be highly motivational for students in grades 6–8. Using technology in writing has these benefits:

● makes topics more real

● links the content areas

- promotes collaboration

- makes inquiry and data sharing more immediate

- promotes higher-level thinking

- deepens students' understanding of research

- helps students recognize that learning in the content areas involves asking questions, not only learning answers

- prompts curiosity and inquiry

- encourages learning in a social context

- promotes discussion at multiple levels (McLaughlin, 2010)

Integrating technology and writing is relatively easy. We can create our own projects or use those developed by others. Students tend to be motivated by the following kinds of integrations:

- **Internet Workshop** (Leu, 2002) is particularly effective for introducing students to websites for an upcoming unit and developing students' background knowledge. During this workshop, students can work individually, with classmates, or with international peers.

- **Internet Project** (Leu, 2001) is a collaborative learning experience between two or more classrooms that takes place over the Internet. We can engage our students in projects designed by others or we can design them ourselves and register them on the Internet to invite others to participate.

- **Internet Inquiry** (Leu & Kinzer, 1999) is a discovery-based process in which students use online sources to research a topic. Students generate important questions and then gather information to answer them. There are five phases of student participation:

  1. generating research questions about the theme or topic being studied

  2. searching the Internet for answers to the questions

  3. analyzing the information found online

  4. choosing a mode in which to present the findings

  5. sharing the results with the class

- **WebQuests** (Dodge, 1995) are inquiry-oriented inquiries that are based on Internet resources preselected by the teacher. WebQuests are designed to engage high-level thinking skills, such as analysis and creativity, rather than basic information-gathering skills.

We can also encourage our students to engage in projects in which they use the writing process and publish their writing electronically. Examples of such projects include electronic publication of alphabet and poetry books produced by the entire class or by individual students. There is no doubt that technology has made and will continue to make important contributions to the teaching and learning of writing. Emerging technologies hold even greater possibilities.

Teaching Writing in the Common Core Classroom

THE COMMON CORE STATE STANDARDS FOR WRITING STATE clear expectations for students to write various types of texts, including narrative, informational, and argumentative texts. In this section, we address each type of writing and suggest ideas to support our teaching.

Narrative Writing

Narrative writing is story-based. This type of writing includes the narrative elements: characters, setting, problem, attempts to resolve the problem, and resolution. Teaching ideas that support narrative writing include Narrative Maps and Retellings.

Narrative Map   The Narrative Map is a graphic organizer that focuses on narrative text structure. Its components typically include characters, setting, problem, attempts to resolve, and resolution. The Narrative Map is often used as the basis for summarizing narrative text and as a structure students use to write their own stories. Figure 6.1 features a completed Narrative Map for Chapter 1 of Jack London's classic, *The Call of the Wild*.

Retelling   The Retelling provides a multifaceted format for summarizing narrative text. Retellings, which are based on the narrative elements, may be oral, written, dramatized, or sketched. Students often find the multiple modes of response to be motivational.

Figure 6.2 features a written Retelling of *The Hunger Games*. In the figure, the student retells Book I.

Student-Authored Stories   Students can write stories in small groups, pairs, or on their own. Students often find working with peers and having access to creative prompts motivational. Students who may not have a strong understanding of the narrative text structure may experience success when they write the story they see in wordless picture books. Author/illustrators, such as David Weisner, tell their stories through their illustrations. If students write what they see, they will easily include all of the narrative elements in their stories.

FIGURE 6.1 ● Completed Narrative Map for Recording Elements of Narrative Text

Text: Chapter 1, "Into the Primitive," *The Call of the Wild* (London, 1903/2012)

Setting	Characters	
Santa Clara Valley Northland	Buck Judge Miller Judge's children	Francois Curly

Problem
Strong dogs are needed for the gold rush in the Northland, and Buck gets kidnapped.

Event 1
Buck grows up in Santa Clara Valley with green pastures.

Event 2
Buck goes hunting and swimming with the judge's children and prides himself on being a pampered house dog.

Event 3
Manuel, the judge's gardener, kidnaps and sells Buck to a strange man.

Event 4
Buck is thrown onto a train, into a ship bound north, where he meets Curly and Francois.

Event 5
Buck arrives in the cold North, where he experiences snow for the first time and gets laughed at by the local people.

Resolution
Buck must wait to learn his fate.

Theme
Buck goes through a life transformation from a house dog to a work dog.

FIGURE 6.2 ● Written Retelling of *The Hunger Games* (Book 1)

The Hunger Games, by Suzanne Collins, is a story about a futuristic utopian society that is controlled by the government, and within the governments control are the lives and the 12 districts of Panem. To manage and keep division of the districts, the government holds a lottery each year. The lottery is called the *reaping*, and two children are chosen from each district to a fight to the death in the Hunger Games. The Hunger Games are televised for everyone to see, and the winner of the games, along with his or her family, is given food and a less restricted life.

The main character, Katniss Everdeen, finds herself becoming a contestant, called a *tribute*, in the Hunger Games. The name of Katniss's younger sister, Prim, is originally called, but Katniss takes her place. Peeta, the son of a baker, is the other name called, and the two children are district 12's tributes. Before the tributes fight in the Hunger Games, they are trained and told how to act in front of the cameras.

During the Hunger Games, Peeta and Katniss form a strong relationship and are portrayed as a couple, even though Katniss is fond of a boy back home named Gale. It was because of Katniss's and Gale's relationship that Katniss is a great hunter and tracker. All through the game, Katniss's hunter instincts are what keep her alive. When Katniss finds herself needing help, she makes an alliance with the youngest tribute, Rue, and is saddened when Rue dies. To show rebellion to the capital, Katniss decorates around Rue's body with flowers.

In the middle of the game, the capital announces that the Hunger Games can have two winners from the same district. After hearing this announcement, Katniss and Peeta become a team and take out all of the other tributes. Once the tributes are down to Katniss and Peeta, the capital takes back the policy of having two winners, and they must now fight each other to the death. Rebelling again against the capital, Katniss and Peeta decide they will commit suicide. Fearing this action will ruin the Hunger Games, the capital quickly intervenes and announces that both Katniss and Peeta are winners. In the end, the two winners are taken back to district 12, and Peeta learns that Katniss's affections were only for the cameras.

Informational Writing

As noted in the Common Core State Standards for Writing, when creating informational writing, students are expected to examine ideas and concepts through the selection, organization, and management of relevant content. Just as narrative writing is based on story elements, informational text is based on informational text structures. Teaching ideas that support writing informational text include K-W-L-S, Bio-Pyramid, and the Informational Text Summary Map.

K-W-L-S When students engage in completing a K-W-L-S, they activate background knowledge, set purposes for reading, and expand their understandings. Students begin by brainstorming what they *know* and what they *want* to know. Then they read the text and record what they *learned*. Finally, they record questions they *still* have about the topic.

Figure 6.3 features a K-W-L-S about the immune system. Please note the K-W-L-S, K-W-D-L, and K-W-H-L are all adaptations of Ogle's classic K-W-L (1986).

Bio-Pyramid The Bio-Pyramid (Macon, 1991) provides an alternative way to summarize a person's life. The pyramid structure accommodates only a particular number of words in each line. The number expands by one in each line after the first. Students can

FIGURE 6.3 ● Completed K-W-L-S Chart about the Immune System

Text: *Biology,* pp. 1036–1042 (Miller & Levine, 2008)

K What I **K**now	W What I **W**ant to Know	L What I **L**earned	S What I **S**till Want to Know
The immune system protects the body from disease. When the skin is broken, infection can enter the body. A fever is a defense mechanism of the immune system.	How does the immune system work? What are some of the ways that the body fights off disease? How does an elevated temperature fight off infections?	The immune system fights infection by producing cells that keep infections out of the body and provides cells to fight infections that have entered the body. Antibodies are the cells that attack pathogens, which are microorganisms that cause disease. Proteins called "interferons" inhibit the growth of a virus by blocking viral replication. An increase in body temperature slows down the growth of pathogens.	Are there different types of viruses that the immune system can fight faster than others? Are there any viruses or bacteria that the immune system cannot fight? What are some ways to strengthen the immune system? Do different people have stronger immune systems than others?

FIGURE 6.4 ● Completed Bio-Pyramid about Clara Barton

Text: "Our history: Founder Clara Barton" (American Red Cross, n.d.)

use the completed Bio-Pyramid as the basis of summary writing. Figure 6.4 features a Bio-Pyramid about Clara Barton.

Informational Text Summary Map   The Informational Text Summary Map is a graphic organizer on which students record information that includes central ideas and details, which can then be used to summarize the text. Figure 6.5 features an example that focuses on the Arctic Sea and global warming.

Argumentative Writing

When writing an argument, our goal is to persuade people to change beliefs they essentially do not want to change. The format for argumentative writing is complex. In this kind of essay, writers not only include information, but, in fully developed arguments, also include a claim, reasons, evidence, anticipated objections, and rebuttal (Toulmin, 1969). Figure 6.6 provides an example of a student-written argumentative essay.

FIGURE 6.5 ● Completed Informational Article Summary Map about the Arctic Sea and Global Warming

Text: "Arctic Sea ice hits record low—Extreme weather to come? (Than, 2012)

Where? Arctic Sea

Who? Researchers

Central Idea: Ice in the Arctic Sea is melting at a significantly fast rate and could cause severe weather events.

Detail 1: Researchers believe that global warming is the cause of sea ice melting faster than normal in the Arctic region during summer melting season.

Detail 2: Climate models used in research indicate that Arctic summers may be ice free sooner than expected—perhaps within the next 30 years.

Detail 3: As sea ice melts, water vapor is produced and heat from the ocean escapes into the atmosphere, contributing to warmer temperatures.

Conclusion: Warmer sea temperatures influence the jet stream and cause extreme weather events, such as heat waves, cold spells, and droughts.

FIGURE 6.6 ● Example of Argumentative Essay

Humans Are Causing Climate Change

For many years, people have been debating the factors of climate change. Some say that humans are the major contributors of climate change, and others say that natural causes are the main factors. It is clear that climate change is a highly debatable issue because it affects humans and the environment around the globe. Nations give a lot of time and money to research and make decisions about climate change. The most discussed factor in climate change is global warming and whether human activities are the major causes. Some scientist and meteorologist disagree with the research on climate change and say it is unreliable. But the majority of scientists from around the world provide strong evidence showing that human activity is the main cause of climate change due to large amounts of greenhouse gases in the atmosphere, glaciers melting and deforestation, and more severe hurricanes, heat waves, and droughts.

(continued)

FIGURE 6.6 ● *(continued)*

Scientists and many national administrations believe that human activity is causing the earth to warm up at astonishing rates. The reason for this increase in global temperature is mainly due to human activities such as burning fossil fuels. It has been reported that carbon dioxide, methane, and nitrous oxide levels are at their highest rates in years. By measuring CO_2 levels in the atmosphere, it is reported that the environment is not absorbing the gas fully, thus more CO_2 is being released into the atmosphere than being absorbed. This action is then raising the earth's temperatures. Some scientists have disputed that the methods and models for measuring CO_2 are flawed and should not be seen as reliable. They also believe that higher CO_2 levels are the result of "carbon sinks" that are found in the oceans, which release CO_2 as a natural occurrence. In addition, water vapor in the atmosphere is another reason for rising temperatures and water vapor comes from natural events like storm systems and shifts in the ocean currents.

Melting glaciers and people dramatically altering land usage such as deforestation are causing climate changes. By using climate change models, it is known that glaciers are melting faster due to rising atmospheric temperatures created by humans. Glaciers have reduced dramatically in size, and these melting glaciers are creating a rise in sea levels. Skeptics for climate models are showing oceans absorbing more CO_2 than in the past. These measurements are being questioned by scientists. Disbelievers in the fact that humans are the major cause of climate change also argue that the role of a more active sun is producing rising atmospheric temperatures.

Supporters agree that climate models show that because greenhouse gasses are warming up our planet, there are more severe hurricanes, heat waves, and droughts. Because of this, warming rainfall in some areas has increased and snow that usually falls in some areas is now rain. Many scientists believe that changes in weather patterns have been induced by human activities of burning fossil fuels. Doubters that humans are the cause of severe weather changes are relying on faulty research. For example, one model stated that the readings were tainted because they were placed too close to artificial heat sources, which gave false readings.

Deciding if human activity is the major cause of climate change is not an easy task. But by looking at all of the scientific evidence presented, it is clear that human activity is the main cause of climate changes. As additional supporting evidence to this rational, major oil companies have provided millions in funding to groups to deny that human activity is the main cause of climate change. The major oil companies want to raise doubts for their own benefits. In the end, it is human activity that is the main cause of climate change; humans are producing large amounts of greenhouse gasses, assisting in the melting of glaciers and contributing to more severe hurricanes, heat waves, and droughts.

Sources:

Climate Change ProCon.org
http://climatechange.procon.org/
Global Warming: Vital Signs of the Planet
http://climate.nasa.gov/causes/
Are Humans Definitely Causing Global Warming?
http://www.guardian.co.uk/environment/2010/dec/30/humans-causing-global-warming

The Discussion Web (Alvermann, 1991) is a teaching idea that provides support for argumentative writing for students in grades 6–8. Students take positions regarding a topic, develop positive and negative arguments, draw a conclusion, and provide a rationale. (See the completed Discussion Web in Chapter 5, p. 111).

Inquiry-Based Research Writing

Researching is an essential skill for students in grades 6–8. Knowing how to generate and respond to meaningful research questions and to use the Internet to its greatest possible advantage to write research projects are essential to this quest.

To avoid engaging students in writing the typical report, we can teach inquiry-based learning (IBL), a project-oriented teaching method that is constructivist in nature (Eick & Reed, 2002). In this process, students ask questions that lead to new understandings, which in turn lead to new questions (Flint & Bomer, 2002). Short and Burke (1996) suggest that inquiry should be viewed as a framework for learning, a context in which students are encouraged to understand at deeper levels.

Inquiry-based learning is viewed as a cyclical process that includes five steps: question, investigate, create, discuss, and reflect. To engage in inquiry, students need to be able to ask good research questions, conduct a viable search, use a variety of quality sources, understand the information they locate, synthesize what they learn, and communicate their findings. Inquiry-based learning benefits students in a variety of ways. It promotes collaborative learning and encourages students to understand at deeper levels. In the process, students become active, motivated participants. They generate questions and access and gather information. They engage in critical and creative thinking, and they analyze and synthesize information. They become problem solvers and understand questioning as a cyclical process. First-Person Experiences and the Rest of the Story are examples of two inquiry-based research projects.

First-Person Experience   In First-Person Experiences (McLaughlin, 2010), students assume the identities of people who played an active role in the event or time period they have chosen to investigate. This inquiry-based project is based on three student-directed decisions. First, students determine the topic they want to research and which person they will become to report their research. Second, they choose the format through which they will share their investigation. Third, they determine the information sources and inquiry techniques they will use to conduct their investigation.

Information sources that students typically use when creating First-Person Experiences include books, articles, newspapers, public documents, interviews, and correspondence—both in print and online. Students' research techniques include personal interviews, surveys, library and Internet searches, experiments, letters of inquiry, field trips, and email.

When teaching students how to create and present First-Person Experiences, we should begin by explaining and modeling the process, emphasizing the critical roles of student choice, reasoning, and planning.

The Rest of the Story   The Rest of the Story (McLaughlin, 2010) is an inquiry-based project that encourages students to go beyond the basic facts generally known about a person, discovery, invention, or event in content area study. Students locate information by using reference books and websites as resources. Technology is involved in this project, as well, in that students choose how to present their investigations to the class. For example, students may prepare a DVD recording of a "news story" reporting the information or a drama that portrays what was learned.

Inventor Alexander Graham Bell is a good example of a topic for the Rest of the Story. Most of us can recall reading his name in a list of inventors as the person who created the telephone. But what is the rest of the story? Consider these little-known facts about the famous inventor:

- Bell was very dedicated to helping the deaf and was a mentor to Helen Keller.
- Bell served as president of the National Geographic Society.
- Bell filed his patent for the telephone just hours before another man filed a similar patent.
- Bell was interested in airplanes and worked with a group that had flown a plane they developed in Canada in 1909.

This is the type of information revealed when students choose to research the rest of the story.

Resources for Lesson Plans

In addition to teaching strategies and applications that focus on writing, we can use lesson plans authored by our peers. A useful source of lesson plans about teaching writing is the website Read-Write-Think (www.readwritethink.org), co-sponsored by the International Reading Association (IRA) and the National Council of Teachers of English (NCTE). This site features teacher-authored lessons and related resources for many different aspects of literacy, including writing.

The following writing lessons, student interactives, and strategy guides are just a few of those available on the Read-Write-Think website for grades 6–8:

- **Student Interactive:** Cube Creator, providing options for Bio Cube, Mystery Cube, Story Cube, and Create-Your-Own Cube (www.readwritethink.org/classroom-resources/student-interactives/cube-30057.html)
- **Lesson Plan:** Examining *Island of the Blue Dolphins* through a Literary Lens (www.readwritethink.org/classroom-resources/lesson-plans/examining-island-blue-dolphins-1068.html)

- **Lesson Plan:** Fighting Injustice by Studying Lessons of the Past (www .readwritethink.org/classroom-resources/lesson-plans/fighting-injustice-studying-lessons-125.html)

- **Student Interactive:** Profile Publisher (www.readwritethink.org/classroom-resources/ student-interactives/profile-publisher-30067.html)

- **Strategy Guide:** Supporting Student Comprehension in Content Area Reading (www.readwritethink.org/professional-development/strategy-guides/supporting-student-comprehension-content-30517.html)

- **Strategy Guide:** Using the RAFT Writing Strategy (www.readwritethink.org/ professional-development/strategy-guides/using-raft-writing-strategy-30625.html)

In the Common Core Classroom

Alexandria is a seventh-grade English language arts teacher. She has been working with her grade-level colleagues in a professional learning community to prepare to implement the Common Core State Standards in their district. One of their emphases has been student writing. After meeting throughout the summer, the planning group decided to begin the school year by focusing on summary writing with their seventh-grade students—not only for its value in helping students learn information in specific disciplines but also for its value in having students collect information from a variety of print and digital sources.

In Alexandria's first rich instructional task, she integrated the CCSS for Reading, Writing, Speaking and Listening, and Language, as follows:

- Reading Informational Text: Standards 2 and 5

- Writing: Standards 2a–f, 4, and 10

- Speaking and Listening: Standard 1a–d

- Language: Standards 1, 3, 4, and 6

After studying the CCSS Writing Standards, Alexandria and her colleagues discussed not only what to teach but also starting points for their instruction. In Alexandria's words:

> We knew what types of writing we needed to teach to help students meet the standards. What took a little longer was determining where we might begin. We engaged in extensive discussions about what our previous year's students knew about writing and could do well. Then we spoke with the teachers of the students we would teach in the fall. We all agreed

that our students were very good at writing stories, but none of us felt confident that our students had been good writers of informational text summaries. So, we decided that would be our starting point.

Next, Alexandria and her colleagues determined teaching ideas and strategies that supported writing informational summaries across the disciplines. They decided to begin by explicitly teaching students the Questions into Paragraphs (QuIP) summarizing technique (McLaughlin, 1987). As Alexandria described, "In our explicit instruction format, we explained, demonstrated, guided, engaged students in independent practice, and reflected."

When using QuIP, students begin by choosing a topic and generating three research questions about it. Then, they use two sources to answer each question. Finally, they write summary paragraphs based on the responses to their questions. A completed QuIP about Neanderthals appears in Figure 6.7.

FIGURE 6.7 ● Completed QuIP Organizer about the Neanderthals

Topic: <u>Neanderthals</u>   **Answers**

Questions	Source 1: http://www.history.com/news/2011/07/19/introducing-your-inner-neanderthal/.	Source 2: http://humanorigins.si.edu/evidence/humanfossils/species/homo-neanderthalensis.
A. How are Neanderthals described?	Neanderthals are close evolutionary cousins to modern humans. They became extinct about 30,000 years ago, but their genes may still live on in European and Asian people today.	Neanderthals, or *Homo neanderthalensis,* are our closest extinct human relatives. They had a large, middle part of their face, angled cheek bones, and a large nose for humidifying and warming cold, dry, air, which was their natural habitat.
B. How did Neanderthals survive?	Scientists have discovered that Neanderthals' bodies were adapted for the cold weather, wore clothes made from animal hides to keep themselves warm, and made sophisticated stone-tipped spears to hunt mammoths in groups. They may even have fashioned their own shoes.	Aside from hunting large game animals, Neanderthals also ate plants, and, when near coastal areas, they ate marine resources such as mollusks, seals, dolphins and fish with thrusting spears. Neanderthals also controlled fire and lived in shelters to stay warm during harsh climates.

● **FIGURE 6.7** ● (*continued*)

| C. Which questions about Neanderthals are still unanswered by scientists today? | Scientists today still do not know exactly why Neanderthals became extinct. Some theories that have been suggested include being absorbed through the Cro-magnum population via interbreeding, losing a competition for resources when modern humans came along, and dying out during the last Ice Age. | There is still much that is unanswered about Neanderthals that scientists are working on solving. These questions include whether there was a correlation between climate change and the extinction of the Neanderthals, the relative contribution of animal and plant sources to the average Neanderthal's diet, and verifying possible evidence of the "symbolic Neanderthal," (i.e. making ornamental or decorative objects, burying the dead). Did these practices just occur in certain populations, and if so, why? |

Neanderthals, or *Homo neanderthalensis*, are close evolutionary cousins to modern humans that died out some 30,000 years ago. Scientists speculate that their genes may still live on today in people of European and Asian descent. They had a large, middle part of their face, angled cheek bones, and a large nose for humidifying and warming cold, dry, air, which was their natural habitat. Scientists have discovered that Neanderthals' bodies were adapted for the cold weather, they wore clothes made from animal hides to keep themselves warm, and they made sophisticated stone-tipped spears to hunt mammoths in groups. Neanderthals also ate plants, and when near coastal areas they ate marine resources such as mollusks, seals, dolphins and fish with thrusting spears. Neanderthals also controlled fire and lived in shelters to stay warm during harsh climates. Although much is known about Neanderthals, there is still a lot that is still unknown, such as why Neanderthals died out. Perhaps it was due to the competition for resources with modern man or the harsh climates of the last Ice Age.

To encourage our students to meet the expectations stated in the CCSS for Writing, we need to provide not only instruction and encouragement but also time—time to collaborate, time to write, time to research, and time to discuss. Meeting the CCSS for Writing is a collaborative venture.

REFERENCES

Alvermann, D. (1991). The discussion web: A graphic aid for learning across the curriculum. *The Reading Teacher, 45*, 92–99.

Dodge, B. (1995). *Some thoughts about WebQuests.* San Diego State University. Retrieved from http://webquest.sdsu.edu/about_webquests.html.

Eick, C. J., & Reed, C. J. (2002). What makes an inquiry oriented science teacher? The influence of learning histories on student teacher role identity and practice. *Science Teacher Education, 86,* 401–416.

Flint, A. S., & Bomer, R. (2002). Inquiry-based instruction. In B. Guzzetti, Ed. *Literacy in America: An encyclopedia of history, theory, and practice,* (Vol. I, pp. 249–251. Santa Barbara, California: ABC-CLIO.

Graham, S., & Hebert, M. (2010). *Writing to read: Evidence for how writing can improve reading—A Carnegie Corporation Time to Act Report.* Washington, DC: Alliance for Excellent Education.

Graham, S., & Perin, D. (2007). *Writing next: Effective strategies to improve writing of adolescents in middle and high schools—A report to the Carnegie Corporation of New York.* Washington, DC: Alliance for Excellent Education.

Leu, D. J. (2001). Internet project: Preparing students for new literacies in a global village. *The Reading Teacher, 54,* 568–572.

Leu, D. J. (2002). Internet workshop: Making time for literacy. *The Reading Teacher, 55,* 466–472.

Leu, D. J., Jr., & Kinzer, C. K. (1999). *Effective reading instruction K–8* (4th ed.). Englewood Cliffs, NJ: Merrill.

Macon, J. M., Bewell, D., & Vogt, M. (1991). *Responses to literature.* Newark, DE: International Reading Association.

McLaughlin, E. M. (1987). QuIP: A writing strategy to improve comprehension of expository structure. *The Reading Teacher, 40,* 650–654.

McLaughlin, M. (2010). *Content area reading: Teaching and learning in an age of multiple literacies.* Boston, MA: Allyn & Bacon.

National Governors Association Center for Best Practices & Council of Chief State School Officers (NGA & CCSSO). (2010a). *Common Core State Standards: English language arts and literacy in history/social studies, science, and technical subjects.* Washington, DC: Authors. Retrieved from www.corestandards.org/assets/CCSSI_ELA%20Standards.pdf.

National Governors Association Center for Best Practices & Council of Chief State School Officers (NGA & CCSSO). (2010b). *Appendix C: Samples of student writing.* In *Common Core State Standards.* Washington, DC: Authors. Retrieved from www.corestandards.org/assets/Appendix_C.pdf.

Ogle, D. (1986). K-W-L: A teaching model that develops active readers of expository text. *The Reading Teacher, 39,* 564–570.

Short, K. G., & Harste, J. C. (with Burke, C.). (1996). *Creating classrooms for authors and inquirers.* Portsmouth, NH: Heinemann.

Sippola, A. E. (1995). K-W-L-S. *The Reading Teacher, 48,* 542 – 543.

Toulmin, S. (1969). *The uses of argument.* Cambridge, UK: Cambridge University Press.

LITERATURE AND INFORMATIONAL TEXTS CITED

American Red Cross. (n.d.) Our history: Founder Clara Barton. *Redcross.org.* Retrieved from www.redcross.org/about-us/history/clara-barton.

Collins, S. (2008). *The hunger games* (Book 1). New York, NY: Scholastic.

London, J. (2012). *The call of the wild.* Rockville, MD: Wildside Press. (Original work published 1903)

Miller, K. R., & Levine, J. S. (2008). *Biology.* Upper Saddle River, NJ: Prentice-Hall.

Than, K. (2012, Aug. 28). Arctic Sea ice hits record low—Extreme weather to come? NationalGeographic.com. Retrieved from http://news.nationalgeographic.com/news/2012/08/120828-arctic-sea-ice-global-warming-record-environment-science.

chapter 7

Curriculum Implications

WHEN WE THINK ABOUT WHAT OUR STUDENTS NEED to know to be successful in meeting the Common Core State Standards (CCSS), we need to consider how the standards connect with our school curriculum. The reality is that not everything that needs to be included in our curriculum is addressed in the Common Core State Standards, and conversely, not everything addressed in the CCSS is currently included in the school curriculum. As noted in Chapter 1, the writers of the Common Core created the standards, but they left decisions about teaching in our hands. The same is true about curriculum development.

Michael Jung/Fotolia

Our goal in this chapter is to situate the CCSS within school curriculum. Overall, we need to ensure that the CCSS are incorporated in but do not replace the existing curriculum. As noted by McLaughlin and Overturf (2012):

> It is important to remember that the Standards delineate student expectations. As the authors of the Common Core State Standards note in the introduction of the document, "The Standards define what all students are expected to know and be able to do, not how teachers should teach" (NGA & CCSSO, 2010, p. 6). This is a powerful statement, because it provides a blueprint for literacy curriculum development in the age of the Common Core. Rather than replacing existing curriculums with the Standards, districts should be striving to integrate the Standards into sound literacy curriculums—student-centered curriculums that include the teaching of reading comprehension strategies. (p. 36)

In this chapter, we begin by examining the curriculum shifts associated with the CCSS. The remainder of the chapter addresses factors involved in implementing the CCSS, including studying the standards, considering CCSS resources from other organizations, integrating the standards in instruction, planning standards-based interdisciplinary units, and planning standards-based lessons.

Curriculum Shifts Related to the CCSS ELA Standards

A VARIETY OF CURRICULUM SHIFTS ARE EXPECTED to emerge in relation to the CCSS. As teachers, it is important for us to view these changes in the context of a comprehensive and integrated English language arts (ELA) curriculum, not in isolation.

The College and Career Readiness (CCR) Anchor Standards and related Common Core State Standards differ from previous state standards. Pearson and Hiebert (2012) suggest that the key differences are close and critical reading, integration of the language arts and content areas, media/research literacy, and text complexity. According to sources that include the New York State Department of Education (2011), the Indiana Department of Education (2011), and educator Robert Rothman (2011), the following ELA curricular shifts will cause us to think about instruction in a new way:

- emphasis on informational text
- discipline literacy
- text complexity
- text-based answers

- speaking and listening
- writing from sources and emphasis on argument
- academic vocabulary

Implementing the CCSS

AS WE IMPLEMENT THE CCSS, WE HAVE MANY things to consider, including how to plan engaging instruction that will motivate students to learn, how to select materials that meet the rigor of the standards yet align with content, how to create lessons to meet a variety of expectations, and how to meet the needs of diverse learners. Then, when initiating our plans, it is critical that we be very well prepared.

To teach students using the Common Core English Language Arts Standards, teachers should plan together in the following ways:

1. Study the standards, including the Appendixes A, B, and C.
2. Consider the CCSS resources provided by other professional organizations.
3. Focus on integrating the ELA standards for instruction.
4. Plan standards-based interdisciplinary units that include formative and summative assessments.
5. Plan standards-based lessons that include formative assessments.

In the remaining sections of this chapter we will consider how to put these guidelines into practice.

Study the Standards, Including the Appendixes

THERE IS NO SUBSTITUTE FOR STUDYING THE CCSS with colleagues (NGA & CCSSO, 2010a). It is important that colleagues come to a common understanding about what the standards mean for curriculum, instruction, and assessment at each grade level. When examining the Standards horizontally, teachers of students in grades 6–8 review the expectations of the CCS for previous grades to determine learning gaps for their sixth, seventh, and eighth grade readers. Teachers of grades 6–8 should also look ahead to the expectations at the next grade to determine how to prepare students for future demands, as well as how to meet the needs of their gifted readers and writers. By studying the Standards vertically as a team, teachers in grades 6–8 can better understand what is expected of their students by the end of that grade level in Reading, Writing, Speaking and Listening, and Language.

In addition to the document that contains the Common Core State Standards (NGA & CCSSO, 2010a), Appendixes A, B, and C are viable resources. Studying Appendix A of the CCSS (NGA & CCSSO, 2010b) will help us understand some of the major research philosophies that underlie the standards and their expectations for students. Appendix A includes research that supports the key elements of the standards and a glossary of key terms. Specifically, it addresses the following topics:

- Reading, with an extensive discussion of text complexity
- Reading Foundational Skills, including phoneme-grapheme correspondences, phonological awareness, and orthography
- Writing, with discussions of the three text types addressed in the standards: argument, informational/explanatory writing, and narrative writing
- Speaking and Listening, addressing the importance of this skill area for students
- Language, including the conventions and knowledge of language and vocabulary

Appendix B (NGA & CCSSO, 2010c) provides text exemplars and sample performance tasks for reading. Studying Appendix B for grades 6, 7, and 8 provides an idea of the levels of text complexity that students are expected to meet in the CCSS. According to the writers of the standards, the texts listed in this appendix are not meant as mandates but rather as texts that "primarily serve to exemplify the level of complexity and quality that the Standards require all students in a given grade band to engage with . . . They expressly do not represent a partial or complete reading list" (NGA & CCSSO, 2010c, p. 2). We should use the titles in Appendix B as models to gauge the complexity of the texts we use in our classrooms. Text exemplars for grades 6–8 are provided for stories, drama, poetry, and informational texts (see Figure 7.1).

Appendix C (NGA & CCSSO, 2010d) provides samples of student writing at each grade level. The samples were created to illustrate particular types of writing required by the CCSS, including argumentative, informative/explanatory, and narrative. Each piece of writing includes a number of annotations explaining how it meets the standards for that grade.

Studying the CCSS horizontally and vertically will deepen our understanding of the standards that our students are expected to meet. Similarly, using Appendixes A, B, and C as resources will increase our understanding of standards-related issues. Interacting with colleagues in studying these materials will foster a common understanding that will serve as the foundation for integrating the CCSS in our teaching.

FIGURE 7.1 ● Text Exemplars for Grades 6–8

Stories

Alcott, Louisa May. *Little Women*
Twain, Mark. *The Adventures of Tom Sawyer*
L'Engle, Madeleine. *A Wrinkle in Time*
Cooper, Susan. *The Dark Is Rising*
Yep, Laurence. *Dragonwings*
Taylor, Mildred D. *Roll of Thunder, Hear My Cry*
Hamilton, Virginia. "The People Could Fly"
Paterson, Katherine. *The Tale of the Mandarin Ducks*
Cisneros, Sandra. "Eleven"
Sutcliff, Rosemary. *Black Ships Before Troy: The Story of the Iliad*

Drama

Fletcher, Louise. *Sorry, Wrong Number*
Goodrich, Frances, and Albert Hackett. *The Diary of Anne Frank: A Play*

Poetry

Longfellow, Henry Wadsworth. "Paul Revere's Ride"
Whitman, Walt. "O Captain! My Captain!"
Carroll, Lewis. "Jabberwocky"
Navajo tradition. "Twelfth Song of Thunder"
Dickinson, Emily. "The Railway Train"
Yeats, William Butler. "The Song of Wandering Aengus"
Frost, Robert. "The Road Not Taken"
Sandburg, Carl. "Chicago"
Hughes, Langston. "I, Too, Sing America"
Neruda, Pablo. "The Book of Questions"
Soto, Gary. "Oranges"
Giovanni, Nikki. "A Poem for My Librarian, Mrs. Long"

Informational Texts

English Language Arts

Adams, John. "Letter on Thomas Jefferson"
Douglass, Frederick. *Narrative of the Life of Frederick Douglass an American Slave, Written by Himself*
Churchill, Winston. "Blood, Toil, Tears and Sweat: Address to Parliament on May 13th, 1940"
Petry, Ann. *Harriet Tubman: Conductor on the Underground Railroad*
Steinbeck, John. *Travels with Charley: In Search of America*

(*continued*)

FIGURE 7.1 • *(continued)*

History/Social Studies

United States. Preamble and First Amendment to the United States Constitution
  (1787, 1791)
Lord, Walter. *A Night to Remember*
Isaacson, Phillip. *A Short Walk through the Pyramids and through the World of Art*
Murphy, Jim. *The Great Fire*
Greenberg, Jan, and Sandra Jordan. *Vincent Van Gogh: Portrait of an Artist*
Partridge, Elizabeth. *This Land Was Made for You and Me: The Life and Songs of
  Woody Guthrie*
Monk, Linda R. *Words We Live By: Your Annotated Guide to the Constitution*
Freedman, Russell. *Freedom Walkers: The Story of the Montgomery Bus Boycott*

Science, Mathematics, and Technical Subjects

Macaulay, David. *Cathedral: The Story of Its Construction*
Mackay, Donald. *The Building of Manhattan*
Enzensberger, Hans Magnus. *The Number Devil: A Mathematical Adventure*
Peterson, Ivars, and Nancy Henderson. *Math Trek: Adventures in the Math Zone*
Katz, John. *Geeks: How Two Lost Boys Rode the Internet out of Idaho*
"Geology." *U*X*L Encyclopedia of Science*
Petroski, Henry. "The Evolution of the Grocery Bag"
"Space Probe." *Astronomy & Space: From the Big Bang to the Big Crunch*
"Elementary Particles." *New Book of Popular Science.*
California Invasive Plant Council. *Invasive Plant Inventory*

Consider CCSS Resources from Other Professional Organizations

WHEN PLANNING CURRICULUM, WE SHOULD CONSIDER ADDITIONAL CCSS resources provided by other professional organizations:

- products of national assessment consortia that may affect guidelines and mandates in our states

- recommendations of the *Revised Publishers' Criteria for the Common Core State Standards in English Language Arts and Literacy, Grades 3–12* (Coleman & Pimentel, 2012) to ensure alignment

- recommendations of the International Reading Association about how to address the learning needs of students in a CCSS-based classroom by clarifying research-based literacy concepts

- recommendations from the writers of the CCSS about how to create text-dependent questions and conduct close reading lessons

- components of the Universal Design for Learning (UDL) framework to help meet the needs of diverse students

- ideas for planning CCSS-based instructional units and lessons that have been suggested by teachers and other literacy leaders in the Tri-State Collaborative (Achieve, 2012)

In the following sections, we review these sources of information and what they recommend for planning a CCSS-based curriculum for grades 6–8. More information about each source can also be found online (see the URL provided for each source).

Assessment Consortia

Two national consortia have designed assessments for English Language Arts and Mathematics Common Core State Standards for grades 3–8 and high school, with implementation set for the school year 2014–2015 (ETS, 2012). The two consortia are the Partnership for Assessment of Readiness for College and Careers (PARCC) (www.parcconline.org) and the Smarter Balanced Assessment Consortium (Smarter Balanced) (www.smarterbalanced.org). Many states that have adopted the CCSS are part of one or the other (and sometimes both) consortia.

Both PARCC and Smarter Balanced have designed assessments to be administered at various times during the school year to gauge students' mastery of the CCSS. PARCC has also created a digital library of resources, including released items, formative assessments, model content frameworks, instructional informative tools and resources, student and educator tutorials and practice tests, scoring training modules, professional development materials, and an interactive report generation system. Similarly, Smarter Balanced offers a digital library of formative tools, processes, and exemplars, released items and tasks, model curriculum units, educator training, professional development tools and resources, scorer training modules, and teacher collaboration tools (ETS, 2012). As we plan curriculum, instruction, and assessment, we need to remember that our states may belong to one of these national consortia. If that is the case, the expectations of these assessments should be key to planning. Updated information about the consortia, their progress, and assessment prototypes can be found on the respective websites.

Two alternate assessment consortia are Dynamic Learning Maps (DLM) (http://dynamiclearningmaps.org) and the National Center and State Collaborative (NCSC) (www.ncscpartners.org). Both consortia have designed assessments based on the CCSS for students with serious cognitive disabilities, who are unable to participate in general state assessments even with appropriate accommodations. In addition, an English language proficiency assessment consortium entitled Assessment Services Supporting ELs Through Technology Systems (ASSETS) (http://assets.wceruw.org) has developed a next-generation, technology-based language assessment system for students in grades K–12 learning English as a second language.

More information about these consortia can be found at the website K–12 Center at ETS (www.k12center.org.)

Publishers' Criteria for the CCSS

Two of the lead authors of the CCSS have provided criteria to guide publishers as they design materials for implementation of the ELA standards. Although the *Revised Publishers' Criteria for the Common Core State Standards in English Language Arts and Literacy, Grades 3–12* (Coleman & Pimentel, 2012) was written for publishers and curriculum developers, many teachers also find the information in this publication helpful as they contemplate teaching students to meet the standards. The *Publishers' Criteria* includes what qualities to consider in text selection, how to develop questions and tasks, how to approach academic vocabulary, and how to design instruction that requires students in grades 3–12 to write to sources and conduct research. (A separate publication provides guidelines for grades K–2.) This publication also includes additional key criteria for students' reading, writing, listening, and speaking. (The *Publishers' Criteria* can be found online at www.corestandards.org/assets/Publishers_Criteria_for_3-12.pdf.)

Literacy Implementation Guidelines

The International Reading Association (IRA, 2012) has published *Literacy Implementation Guidance for the ELA Common Core State Standards.* This document was designed to clarify literacy issues related to the CCSS and addresses these topics: use of challenging text, foundational skills, reading comprehension, vocabulary, writing, disciplinary literacy, and diverse learners. (This IRA document is available online at www.reading.org/general/AboutIRA/white-papers/ela-common-core-standards.aspx.)

Creating Text-Dependent Questions and Close Reading Lessons

One of the major instructional shifts in the ELA standards is that students are expected to provide text-based answers to text-dependent questions. This means that the questions must be based on the text, not on students' personal experiences. In addition, the answers must either be literal interpretations of the text or be logically inferred from the text—not from students' own ideas. As a result of this instructional shift, students have "rich and rigorous conversations which are dependent on a common text" and they write from sources "using evidence to inform or make an argument" (New York State Department of Education, 2011).

Assessment of students' reading, writing, and thinking about complex texts generally begins in third grade and is expected of all students. To meet this expectation, we need to create text-dependent questions and facilitate close reading lessons that engage students in rigorous text-based conversations about complex texts. Professional development materials and examples of text-dependent questions and close reading lessons for grades 6–8 can be found on the website Achieve the Core (www.achievethecore.org) in the section entitled "Steal These Tools."

Universal Design for Learning

The writers of the CCSS state explicitly that the standards do not describe how to address students with disabilities, English language learners, or students who are advanced (NGA & CCSSO, 2010a, p. 6). However, there are brief additions to the CCSS that describe their application to students with disabilities (NGA & CCSSO, 2010e) and to students who are English language learners (NGA & CCSSO, 2010f). (See the References for the URLs of these documents, or go to www.corestandards.org/the-standards/download-the-standards.)

The document "Application to Students with Disabilities" (NGA & CCSSO, 2010e) includes a reference to the principles of Universal Design for Learning (UDL). Actually, UDL is a framework for designing curriculum for *all* students, including students with disabilities, English language learners, struggling readers and writers, and gifted students to reduce barriers that prohibit learning (CAST, 2012). The overarching idea of UDL is that because every student learns differently, the curriculum should be designed to accommodate the needs of diverse learners, rather than designed for average learners and adapted for other learners after the fact. Within the UDL framework, students gain knowledge, skills and strategies, and enthusiasm for learning. Instruction should provide students with multiple means of representation (i.e., presenting information and content in different ways), multiple means of action and expression (i.e., differentiating the ways that students can express what they know), and multiple means of engagement (i.e., stimulating students' interest and motivation for learning).

Although UDL was created to assist in curriculum design for diverse learners, teachers find it helpful when planning units and lessons in Common Core classrooms. All students are expected to master the CCSS, which means teachers must plan instruction to meet the needs of individual students.

More information about UDL can be found at the website of the National Center on Universal Design for Learning (www.udlcenter.org).

Tri-State Quality Review Rubric for Lessons and Units

Educators from Massachusetts, New York, and Rhode Island (facilitated by Achieve, Inc.) collaborated to create the *Tri-State Quality Review Rubric for Lessons and Units: ELA/Literacy (Grades 3–5) and ELA (Grades 6–12)* (Achieve, 2012). This rubric was designed to evaluate ELA CCSS lessons and units to ensure rigor and alignment to the standards. The rubric can be used to design instruction and evaluate it.

The "CCSS-Based Thematic Unit Checklist" and the "CCSS-Based Lesson Checklist" that appear in Figures 7.2 and 7.3 were both adapted from the *Tri-State Quality Review Rubric,* version 4.1 (Achieve, 2012). The most recent version of the rubric can be found on the Achieve website in the section "EQuIP" (www.achieve.org/EQuIP).

FIGURE 7.2 ● CCSS-Based Thematic Unit Checklist: Grades 6–8

Alignment to the Rigor of the CCSS

Focus of Unit

Y   N   1. Does the unit target a set of grades 6–8 CCSS ELA/Literacy standards?

Y   N   2. Does the unit include a clear and explicit purpose for instruction?

Y   N   3. Is the unit planned to build both students' content knowledge and their understanding of reading and writing in social studies, the arts, and science or technical subjects?

Y   N   4. Does the unit address instructional expectations, and is it easy to understand and use?

Text Selection

Y   N   5. Does the unit include texts within the grade-level text complexity band that present vocabulary, syntax, text structures, levels of meaning/purpose, and other qualitative characteristics similar to those of the CCSS grade-level exemplars in Appendixes A and B? (Grade 8 is the high end of the text complexity band for grades 6–8.)

Y   N   6. Does the unit include a balance of informational and literary texts?

Instructional Focus

Y   N   7. Is the unit planned to integrate reading, writing, and speaking and listening so that students apply and synthesize their advancing literacy skills?

Y   N   8. Is the unit planned to cultivate students' interest and engagement in reading, writing, and speaking about texts?

Y   N   9. Is the unit planned to provide for authentic learning, application of literacy skills, and student-directed inquiry, analysis, evaluation, and reflection?

Y   N   10. Is the unit planned to include a progression of learning in which concepts and skills advance and deepen over time?

Y   N   11. Do unit lessons gradually remove supports, requiring students to demonstrate their independent capacities?

Y   N   12. Do unit lessons integrate targeted instruction in such areas as grammar and conventions, writing strategies, and discussion roles for grades 6–8?

(continued)

FIGURE 7.2 ● *(continued)*

Key Areas for Instruction

Reading

Y   N   13. Does the unit include learning experiences that require students to read text(s) closely, examine textual evidence, and discern the meaning as a central focus of instruction?

Y   N   14. Does the unit focus on comprehending challenging sections of text(s) and engage students in a productive struggle to understand them through the use of discussion questions and other supports that build toward independence?

Y   N   15. Does the unit include learning experiences that have students read a progression of complex texts drawn from the appropriate grade-level band? Does it provide text-centered learning experiences that are sequenced, scaffolded, and supported to advance students toward independent reading of complex texts at the college- and career-readiness level?

Y   N   16. Does the unit provide opportunities for students to build knowledge about a topic or subject through analysis of a coherent selection of strategically sequenced, discipline-specific texts?

Y   N   17. Does the unit include independent reading based on students' choices and interests to build stamina, confidence, and motivation? Does it indicate how students are accountable for independent reading?

Writing

Y   N   18. Does the unit include learning experiences that expect students to draw evidence from texts to produce clear and coherent writing that informs, explains, or expresses an opinion supported by reasons and evidence in various forms (e.g., notes, summaries, short responses, formal essays)?

Y   N   19. Does the unit include a balance of on-demand and process writing (e.g., multiple drafts and revisions over time) and short, focused research projects, incorporating digital texts when appropriate?

Speaking and Listening

Y   N   20. Does the unit include learning experiences that engage students in rich and rigorous evidence-based discussions through a sequence of specific thought-provoking and text-dependent questions (including, when applicable, illustrations, charts, diagrams, audio/video, and media)?

(continued)

FIGURE 7.2 ● *(continued)*

Language

Y   N   21. Does the unit include learning experiences that focus on building students' academic vocabulary in context throughout instruction?

Technology

Y   N   22. Does the unit use technology and media to deepen students' learning and draw attention to evidence in texts as appropriate?

Responsiveness to Varied Student Needs

Y   N   23. Does the unit provide *all* students with multiple opportunities to engage with texts of appropriate complexity for the grade level and include appropriate scaffolding so that students correctly experience the complexity of the texts?

Y   N   24. Does the unit integrate appropriate supports in reading, writing, listening, and speaking for students who are English language learners, have disabilities, or read well below the grade-level text band?

Y   N   25. Does the unit provide extensions and/or more advanced texts for students who read well above the grade-level text band?

Assessments

Y   N   26. Do assessments in the unit elicit direct, observable evidence of the degree to which a student can independently demonstrate the major targeted grade-level CCSS standards with appropriately complex texts?

Y   N   27. Do assessments in the unit assess student proficiency using methods that are unbiased and accessible to all students?

Y   N   28. Do assessments in the unit include aligned rubrics or assessment guidelines that provide sufficient guidance for interpreting student performance?

Y   N   29. Do assessments in the unit use varied modes, including a range of pre-, formative, summative, and self-assessment measures?

Note: Adapted from *Tri-state quality review rubric for lessons and units: ELA/Literacy (grades 3–5) and ELA (grades 6–12),* version 4.1 (Achieve, 2012).

FIGURE 7.3 ● CCSS-Based Lesson Checklist: Grades 6–8

Alignment to the Rigor of the CCSS

Focus of Lesson

Y   N   1. Does the lesson target a set of grades 6–8 CCSS ELA/Literacy standards?

Y   N   2. Does the lesson include a clear and explicit purpose for instruction?

Y   N   3. Is the lesson planned to build both students' content knowledge and their understanding of reading and writing in social studies, the arts, and science or technical subjects?

Text Selection

Y   N   4. Does the lesson include a text within the grade-level text complexity band that presents vocabulary, syntax, text structures, levels of meaning/purpose, and other qualitative characteristics similar to those of the CCSS grade-level exemplars in Appendixes A and B? (Grade 8 is the high end of the text complexity band for grades 6–8.)

Instructional Focus

Y   N   5. Is the lesson planned to integrate two or more standards so that students apply and synthesize their advancing literacy skills?

Y   N   6. Is the lesson planned to cultivate students' interest and engagement in reading, writing, or speaking about texts?

Y   N   7. Is the lesson planned to provide for authentic learning, application of literacy skills, and student-directed inquiry, analysis, evaluation, and reflection?

Y   N   8. Does the lesson provide supports where necessary but gradually remove them, requiring students to demonstrate their independent capacities?

Key Areas for Instruction

Does the lesson focus on at least *one* of these key areas of instruction in the ELA CCSS?

Y   N   9. Does the lesson focus on reading text closely, examining textual evidence, and discerning deep meaning?

Y   N   10. Does the lesson focus on facilitating a rich and rigorous evidence-based discussion through a sequence of specific, thought-provoking, and text-dependent questions (including, when applicable, illustrations, charts, diagrams, audio/video, and media)?

(continued)

FIGURE 7.3 ● (*continued*)

Y   N   11. Does the lesson focus on students drawing evidence from the text to produce clear and coherent writing that informs, explains, or supports an opinion in various written forms (e.g., notes, summaries, short responses, formal essays)?

Y   N   12. Does the lesson focus on building students' academic vocabulary in context?

Responsiveness to Varied Student Learning Needs

Y   N   13. Does the lesson provide *all* students with multiple opportunities to engage with texts of appropriate complexity for the grade level and include appropriate scaffolding so that students correctly experience the complexity of the texts?

Y   N   14. Does the lesson integrate appropriate supports in reading, writing, and/ or listening and speaking for students who are English language learners, have disabilities, or read well below the grade-level text band?

Y   N   15. Does the lesson provide extensions and/or more advanced text for students who read well above the grade-level text band?

Assessments

Y   N   16. Do assessments align with the purpose of the lesson (pre-, formative, summative, or self-assessment)?

Y   N   17. Do assessments in the lesson assess student proficiency using methods that are unbiased and accessible to all students?

Y   N   18. Do assessments in the lesson include aligned rubrics or assessment guidelines that provide sufficient guidance for interpreting student performance?

Y   N   19. Do assessments in the lesson elicit direct, observable evidence of the degree to which a student can independently demonstrate the major targeted grade-level CCSS standards with appropriately complex texts?

Note: Adapted from *Tri-state quality review rubric for lessons and units: ELA/Literacy (grades 3–5) and ELA (grades 6–12),* version 4.1 (Achieve, 2012).

Integrating the ELA Standards in Instruction

THE ELA STANDARDS WERE BUILT ON AN INTEGRATED model of literacy and designed to be connected and interwoven. The ELA CCSS document states, "Although the Standards are divided into Reading, Writing, Speaking and Listening, and Language strands for conceptual clarity, the processes of communication are closely connected, as reflected throughout this document" (NGA & CCSSO, 2010a, p. 4). The expectation is that the CCSS should not be taught in isolation; rather, they should be integrated when planning instruction and assessment. In fact, the writers of the CCSS state unambiguously, "While the Standards delineate specific expectations in reading, writing, speaking, listening, and language, each standard need not be a separate focus for instruction and assessment. Often, several standards can be addressed by a single rich task" (NGA & CCSSO, 2010a, p. 5).

When planning for instruction, we should look for the obvious connections between and among standards to create such rich instructional tasks. For example, suppose we are planning a reading task in which sixth-grade students will read an informational text. We can address several standards for Reading Informational Text at the same time by considering these standards for sixth grade (NGA & CCSSO, 2010a):

- **RI.6.1:** Cite textual evidence to support analysis of what the text says explicitly as well as inferences drawn from the text.
- **RI.6.2:** Determine a central idea of a text and how it is conveyed through particular details; provide a summary of the text distinct from personal opinions or judgments.
- **RI.6.7:** Integrate information presented in different media or formats (e.g., visually, quantitatively) as well as in words to develop a coherent understanding of a topic or issue.

In the same lesson, we can facilitate discussion of the text and ask students to share their findings. Doing so allows us to integrate these standards for Speaking and Listening within our rich instructional task (NGA & CCSSO, 2010a):

- **SL.6.1:** Engage effectively in a range of collaborative discussions (one-on-one, in groups, and teacher-led) with diverse partners on *grade 6 topics, texts, and issues,* building on others' ideas and expressing their own clearly.
- **SL.6.4:** Present claims and findings, sequencing ideas logically and using pertinent descriptions, facts, and details to accentuate main ideas or themes; use appropriate eye contact, adequate volume, and clear pronunciation.

If we ask students to respond to a text by writing about it, we can also incorporate these Writing standards in the task (NGA & CCSSO, 2010a):

- **W.6.2:** Write informative/explanatory texts to examine a topic and convey ideas, concepts, and information through the selection, organization, and analysis of relevant content.
- **W.6.9:** Draw evidence from literary or informational texts to support analysis, reflection, and research.

Furthermore, we can include the following Language standards within the writing and speaking tasks:

- **L.6.1:** Demonstrate command of the conventions of standard English grammar and usage when writing or speaking.

- **L.6.2:** Demonstrate command of the conventions of standard English capitalization, punctuation, and spelling when writing.

- **L.6.6:** Acquire and use accurately grade-appropriate general academic and domain-specific words and phrases; gather vocabulary knowledge when considering a word or phrase important to comprehension or expression.

When we integrate multiple standards in our lessons, our students have a much richer experience and a better understanding of how reading, writing, speaking and listening, language, and vocabulary are interrelated.

Planning Standards-based Interdisciplinary Units

TO TEACH IN A WAY THAT INTEGRATES THE CCSS AND CONTENT, meets the needs of all learners, and engages and motivates students, we can plan integrated interdisciplinary instruction. Planning an integrated CCSS-based interdisciplinary unit means examining the curriculum and looking for ways to connect language arts and other content areas, such as science, social studies, the arts, and mathematics. It means considering the needs of students and designing engaging instruction in which students have choices. It also means providing a variety of assessments for a variety of purposes.

As we plan standards-based interdisciplinary units, there are several questions we should consider:

How can we design a Common Core interdisciplinary unit? A CCSS-based instructional unit should target specific content and related ELA Standards. These are the standards that will be taught and assessed throughout the unit. The unit should include clear and explicit purposes for instruction. It should also be planned to build both students' content knowledge and their understanding of reading and writing in the disciplines (i.e., social studies, the arts, science, or technical subjects) through the coherent selection of appropriate texts.

How should we select texts for the unit? In grades 6–8, there is an emphasis on reading informational texts, but both literature and informational texts can be integrated in disciplinary units. For example, when planning a unit on poetry, we can include informational texts about the life and writing style of the poet, historical events that may have influenced the poem, or scientific information about the topic of the poem. When planning a unit on content, such World War II, we can include both informational texts and literature about the Holocaust and other topics related to the war. Doing so enriches students' thinking and helps them understand more deeply.

The CCSS also have expectations for students to read complex texts closely and discuss text-dependent questions as they analyze a text. Complex texts to be read closely should be selected within the grade-level text complexity band that presents vocabulary, syntax, text structures, levels of meaning/purpose, and other qualitative characteristics similar to the CCSS grade-level exemplars presented in Appendix A (NGA & CCSSO, 2010b) and Appendix B (NGA & CCSSO, 2010c). In addition, a variety of levels of texts about the unit topic and related issues should be available in the classroom for research and self-selected reading at students' independent levels.

What should be the focus of instruction?   A CCSS-based instructional unit should be planned to integrate reading, writing, speaking and listening, and language so that students apply and synthesize their advancing literacy skills. Motivation is a key part of learning, and learning experiences should be planned that cultivate students' interest and engagement in reading, writing, and speaking about texts. Opportunities should be provided for authentic learning, in which students have choices and engage in real tasks. We should also provide plenty of time for student-directed inquiry, analysis, evaluation, and reflection.

The interdisciplinary unit should be planned to show a progression of learning, recognizing how concepts and skills advance and deepen over time. The lessons in the unit should be sequenced so we can provide scaffolding as necessary, but we should also be able to gradually release responsibility for learning to students by progressively lessening supports and encouraging students to demonstrate their independent capacities. Unit lessons should also integrate targeted instruction in such areas as grammar and conventions, writing strategies, discussion roles, and all of the foundational aspects of reading for grades 6–8.

What are key considerations for each strand of the ELA Standards?   In Reading, the central focus of instruction in the unit should include learning experiences in which students read texts closely, examine textual evidence, and construct meaning. There should also be a focus on comprehending short complex texts and engaging students in close reading, during which students use text-based discussion questions and other supports that build independence. The unit should include learning experiences that involve students' reading a progression of complex texts from the appropriate grade-level band. The unit should provide opportunities for students to build knowledge about a topic or subject through analysis of a coherent selection of strategically sequenced, discipline-specific texts. Students should also have opportunities for independent reading based on their choices and interests to build stamina, confidence, and motivation.

In Writing, student expectations should include creating narrative and informational texts, including arguments that are clear and coherent. The unit should feature a balance of informal (e.g., notes, summaries, and journal entries) and formal writing (e.g., research projects), incorporating digital texts as appropriate.

In Speaking and Listening, the unit should include learning experiences that engage students in rich and rigorous evidence-based discussions. Such discussions can be initiated by asking a sequence of specific, thought-provoking, and text-dependent questions, including, when applicable, illustrations, charts, diagrams, audio/video, and media.

In Language, the unit should include learning experiences that focus on building students' academic vocabulary in context throughout instruction.

The unit should also integrate technology and a variety of media to deepen students' learning and draw attention to evidence in texts as appropriate.

How can we be responsive to the needs of diverse learners? A unit should provide *all* students with multiple opportunities to read texts of suitable complexity for the grade level and include appropriate scaffolding as necessary. Instruction should integrate appropriate supports in reading, writing, and listening and speaking for English language learners, students with disabilities, and students who read well below the grade-level text band. The unit should also include extensions and/or more advanced texts for students who read well above the grade-level text band.

How should we plan assessments? Varied modes of assessments should be used in the unit, including a range of pre-, formative, summative, and self-assessment measures. Assessments should elicit direct, observable evidence of the degree to which a student independently demonstrates achievement of the targeted grade level CCSS standards. The assessments in the unit should measure students' proficiency using methods that are unbiased and accessible to all students. Assessments should include Common Core-aligned checklists or rubrics as appropriate to the task.

An example of an interdisciplinary Common Core State Standards-based unit for grades 6–8 is provided in the Appendix of this volume. The unit focuses on the human impact on climate change.

Final Thoughts

PLANNING TO IMPLEMENT THE COMMON CORE STATE STANDARDS is not easy, but it is imperative if every student is to be college and career ready. Each of us is responsible for a piece in the larger mosaic of Common Core implementation. Studying the standards, reading and discussing recommendations from organizations and states involved in implementation, learning how to integrate standards, and designing Standards-based interdisciplinary units, Standards-based lessons, and daily schedules for implementation are all part of what we need to do to ensure our students successfully meet the expectations of the Common Core.

REFERENCES

Achieve. (2012). *Tri-state quality review rubric for lessons and units: ELA/Literacy (grades 3–5) and ELA (grades 6–12),* version 4.1. *Achieve.* Retrieved from http://www.achieve.org/files/TriStateELA_LiteracyRubric1pageoverviewv4.1%20071712CC%20BY.pdf.

CAST. (2012). About UDL. *National Center on Universal Design for Learning, at CAST.* Retrieved from http://www.udlcenter.org/aboutudl/whatisudl.

Coleman, D., & Pimentel, S. (2012). *Revised publishers' criteria for the Common Core State Standards in English language arts and literacy, grades 3–12.* Washington, DC: National Governors Association, Council of Chief State School Officers, Achieve, Council of Great City Schools, and National Association of State Boards of Education. Retrieved from http://www.corestandards.org/assets/Publishers_Criteria_for_3-12.pdf.

Educational Testing Service (ETS). (2012, April). *Coming together to raise student achievement: New assessments for the Common Core State Standards.* Center for K–12 Assessment and Performance Management at ETS. Retrieved from http://k12center.org/rsc/pdf/Coming_Together_April_2012_Final.PDF.

Indiana Department of Education. (2011, Aug. 29). *Four major shifts in literacy* [Video]. Common Core. Retrieved from www.doe.in.gov/achievement/curriculum/four-major-shifts-literacy.

International Reading Association (IRA). (2012). *Literacy implementation guidance for the ELA Common Core State Standards.* Common Core State Standards (CCSS) Committee. Retrieved from http://www.reading.org/Libraries/association-documents/ira_ccss_guidelines.pdf.

McLaughlin, M., & Overturf, B. J. (2012). The Common Core and reading comprehension: What's in the standards and what we need to teach. *Reading Today, 30*(2), 35–36.

National Governors Association Center for Best Practices & Council of Chief State School Officers (NGA & CCSSO). (2010a). *Common Core State Standards: English language arts and literacy in history/social studies, science, and technical subjects.* Washington, DC: Authors. Retrieved from http://www.corestandards.org/assets/CCSSI_ELA%20Standards.pdf.

National Governors Association Center for Best Practices & Council of Chief State School Officers (NGA & CCSSO). (2010b). Appendix A: Research supporting key elements of the standards and glossary of key terms. *Common Core State Standards.* Washington, DC: Authors. Retrieved from http://www.corestandards.org/assets/Appendix_A.pdf.

National Governors Association Center for Best Practices & Council of Chief State School Officers (NGA & CCSSO). (2010c). Appendix B: Text exemplars and sample performance tasks. *Common Core State Standards.* Washington, DC: Authors. Retrieved from http://www.corestandards.org/assets/Appendix_B.pdf.

National Governors Association Center for Best Practices & Council of Chief State School Officers (NGA & CCSSO). (2010d). Appendix C: Samples of student writing. *Common Core State Standards.* Washington, DC: Authors. Retrieved from http://corestandards.org/assets/Appendix_C.pdf.

National Governors Association Center for Best Practices & Council of Chief State School Officers (NGA & CCSSO). (2010e). Application to students with disabilities. *Common Core State Standards.* Washington, DC: Authors. Retrieved from http://www.corestandards.org/assets/application-to-students-with-disabilities.pdf.

National Governors Association Center for Best Practices & Council of Chief State School Officers (NGA & CCSSO). (2010f). Application of Common Core State Standards for English language learners. *Common Core State Standards.* Washington, DC: Authors. Retrieved from http://www.corestandards.org/assets/application-for-english-learners.pdf.

New York State Department of Education. (2011). Common Core instructional shifts. *EngageNY.* Retrieved from http://engageny.org/resource/common-core-shifts/.

Pearson, P. D., & Hiebert, E. H. (2012). Understanding the Common Core State Standards. In L. M. Morrow, T. Shanahan, & K. K. Wixson (Eds.), *Teaching with the Common Core Standards for English Language Arts, PreK–2* (pp. 1–21) New York, NY: Guilford Press.

Rothman, R. (2011). *Something in common: The Common Core Standards and the next chapter.* Cambridge, MA: Harvard Education Press.

Human Impact on Climate Change
An Interdisciplinary Unit for Grades 6–8

HUMAN IMPACT ON CLIMATE CHANGE IS AN INTERDISCIPLINARY unit designed for grades 6–8. In this unit, which was designed to last approximately three or four weeks, learning has been integrated across multiple disciplines: English language arts, science, social studies, and the arts (art, music and drama). In addition, numerous Common Core State Standards (CCSS) for grades 6–8 are incorporated to support the creation of rich instructional tasks. (Note that when specific CCSS are cited, they are grade 8 standards.)

Chagin/Fotolia

Human Impact on Climate Change

TOPIC: Climate change

GRADE LEVELS: Grades 6–8

DURATION: 3–4 weeks

DISCIPLINES: English Language Arts, Science, Social Studies, and the Arts (Art, Drama, and Music)

ENDURING UNDERSTANDING: People have powerful influences on the world in which they live.

ESSENTIAL UNDERSTANDINGS

1. Climate change has been occurring for a period of time.
2. Understanding of the climate system is improved through observations, theoretical studies, and actions.
3. Human activities are impacting the climate system.
4. Climate change will have consequences for the Earth and its people.

GUIDING QUESTIONS

1. Why is climate change considered to be a global problem?
2. How have humans contributed to climate change?

ELA STATE STANDARDS

The following Common Core English Language Arts Standards will be integrated throughout the Unit:

Reading: Literature

RL.8.1:   Cite the textual evidence that most strongly supports an analysis of what the text says explicitly as well as inferences drawn from the text.

RL.8.5:   Compare and contrast the structure of two or more texts and analyze how the differing structure of each text contributes to its meaning and style.

Reading: Informational Text

RI.8.1:   Cite the textual evidence that most strongly supports an analysis of what the text says explicitly as well as inferences drawn from the text.

RI.8.2:   Determine a central idea of a text and analyze its development over the course of the text, including its relationship to supporting ideas; provide an objective summary of the text.

RI.8.7:   Evaluate the advantages and disadvantages of using different mediums (e.g., print or digital text, video, multimedia) to present a particular topic or idea.

RI.8.8:   Delineate and evaluate the argument and specific claims in a text, assessing whether the reasoning is sound and the evidence is relevant and sufficient; recognize when irrelevant evidence is introduced.

Writing

W.8.1a–e: Write arguments to support claims with clear reasons and relevant evidence.

     a. Introduce claim(s), acknowledge and distinguish the claim(s) from alternate or opposing claims, and organize the reasons and evidence logically.

     b. Support claim(s) with logical reasoning and relevant evidence, using accurate, credible sources and demonstrating an understanding of the topic or text.

     c. Use words, phrases, and clauses to create cohesion and clarify the relationships among claim(s), counterclaims, reasons, and evidence.

     d. Establish and maintain a formal style.

     e. Provide a concluding statement or section that follows from and supports the argument presented.

W.8.2a–f: Write informative/explanatory texts to examine a topic and convey ideas, concepts, and information through the selection, organization, and analysis of relevant content.

     a. Introduce a topic clearly, previewing what is to follow; organize ideas, concepts, and information into broader categories; include formatting (e.g., headings), graphics (e.g., charts, tables), and multimedia when useful to aiding comprehension.

     b. Develop the topic with relevant, well-chosen facts, definitions, concrete details, quotations, or other information and examples.

     c. Use appropriate and varied transitions to create cohesion and clarify the relationships among ideas and concepts.

     d. Use precise language and domain-specific vocabulary to inform about or explain the topic.

     e. Establish and maintain a formal style.

     f. Provide a concluding statement or section that follows from and supports the information or explanation presented.

W.8.4:   Produce clear and coherent writing in which the development, organization, and style are appropriate to task, purpose, and audience.

W.8.5:   With some guidance and support from peers and adults, develop and strengthen writing as needed by planning, revising, editing, rewriting, or trying a new approach, focusing on how well purpose and audience have been addressed.

W.8.6:   Use technology, including the Internet, to produce and publish writing and present the relationships between information and ideas efficiently as well as to interact and collaborate with others.

W.8.7:   Conduct short research projects to answer a question (including a self-generated question), drawing on several sources and generating additional related, focused questions that allow for multiple avenues of exploration.

W.8.8:   Gather relevant information from multiple print and digital sources, using search terms effectively; assess the credibility and accuracy of each source; and quote or paraphrase the data and conclusions of others while avoiding plagiarism and following a standard format for citation.

W.8.10:   Write routinely over extended time frames (time for research, reflection, and revision) and shorter time frames (a single sitting or a day or two) for a range of discipline-specific tasks, purposes, and audiences.

Speaking and Listening

SL.8.1:   Engage effectively in a range of collaborative discussions (one-on-one, in groups, and teacher-led) with diverse partners on *grade 8 topics and texts,* building on others' ideas and expressing their own clearly.

SL.8.2:   Analyze the purpose of information presented in diverse media and formats (e.g., visually, quantitatively, orally) and evaluate the motives (e.g., social, commercial, political) behind its presentation.

SL.8.3:   Delineate a speaker's argument and specific claims, evaluating the soundness of the reasoning and relevance and sufficiency of the evidence and identifying when irrelevant evidence is introduced.

SL.8.4:   Present claims and findings, emphasizing salient points in a focused, coherent manner with relevant evidence, sound valid reasoning, and well-chosen details; use appropriate eye contact, adequate volume, and clear pronunciation.

SL.8.5:   Integrate multimedia and visual displays into presentations to clarify information, strengthen claims and evidence, and add interest.

Language

L.8.1:   Demonstrate command of the conventions of standard English grammar and usage when writing or speaking.

L.8.2: Demonstrate command of the conventions of standard English capitalization, punctuation, and spelling when writing.

L.8.3: Use knowledge of language and its conventions when writing, speaking, reading, or listening.

L.8.4 a–d: Determine or clarify the meaning of unknown and multiple-meaning words or phrases based on *grade 8 reading and content,* choosing flexibly from a range of strategies.

   a. Use context (e.g., the overall meaning of a sentence or paragraph; a word's position or function in a sentence) as a clue to the meaning of a word or phrase.

   b. Use common, grade-appropriate Greek or Latin affixes and roots as clues to the meaning of a word (e.g., *precede, recede, secede*).

   c. Consult general and specialized reference materials (e.g., dictionaries, glossaries, thesauruses), both print and digital, to find the pronunciation of a word or determine or clarify its precise meaning or its part of speech.

   d. Verify the preliminary determination of the meaning of a word or phrase (e.g., by checking the inferred meaning in context or in a dictionary).

L.8.6: Acquire and use accurately grade-appropriate general academic and domain-specific words and phrases; gather vocabulary knowledge when considering a word or phrase important to comprehension or expression.

SCIENCE CONNECTION

Next Generation Science Standard The topic "Weather and Climate" is one of six earth and space science topics in the Next Generation Science Standards (NSTA, 2013). The related performance standards for middle school students are based on a set of foundational concepts, practices, and ideas, including Disciplinary Core Ideas. In addition, the standards reflect not only discipline-specific knowledge but also "societally relevant aspects" of science.

   As indicated in the standard that follows (as well as its associated Disciplinary Core Idea), student expectations for the topic "Weather and Climate" include an understanding of global climate change:

MS-ESS3-5: Ask questions to clarify evidence of the factors that have caused the rise in global temperatures over the past century. [*Clarification Statement:* Examples of factors include human activities (such as fossil fuel combustion, cement production, and agricultural activity) and natural processes (such as changes in incoming solar radiation or volcanic activity). Examples of evidence can include tables, graphs, and maps of global and regional temperatures, atmospheric levels of gases such as carbon dioxide and methane, and the rates of human activities.

Emphasis is on the major role that human activities play in causing the rise in global temperatures.]

Disciplinary Core Idea: ESS3.D: Global Climate Change: Human activities, such as the release of greenhouse gases from burning fossil fuels, are major factors in the current rise in Earth's mean surface temperature (global warming). Reducing the level of climate change and reducing human vulnerability to whatever climate changes do occur depend on the understanding of climate science, engineering capabilities, and other kinds of knowledge, such as understanding of human behavior and on applying that knowledge wisely in decisions and activities. (MS-ESS3-5)

UNIT EXTENSIONS

Science

1. Invite students to engage in Internet Inquiry (Leu & Leu, 1999) to research a self-selected aspect of climate change. *Recommended resource:* http://epa.gov/climatechange/kids/index.html.

2. Encourage students to write and sketch problems resulting from climate change. They record their thoughts about how to reduce the effects of climate change on the right side of a piece of paper and sketch their representation of thoughts on the left side of the paper. Then they complete Discussion Webs and use them as the basis of a series of debates. *Recommended resource:* www.globalchange.gov.

3. Engage students in First-Person Experiences (McLaughlin, 2010a). Students make a series of choices concerning climate change-related topics, including which topic they will address, the research questions, the sources, and the mode of presentation.

4. Engage students in creating investigative journals in which they records questions about the characteristics of climate change. Students conduct research, write a summary, and reflect on their findings. *Recommended resource:* http://epa.gov/climatechange/kids/index.html.

5. Encourage students to engage in "Critical Literacy in Action: Multimodal Texts on Global Warming" (Grades 6–8). Four 45- to 60-minute sessions. *Recommended resource:* http://www.readwritethink.org/classroom-resources/lesson-plans/critical-literacy-action-multimodal-1139.html.

   Students apply specific comprehension strategies to multimodal texts as they investigate and interrogate the effects and possible causes of global warming. Students explore global warming through a variety of photographs, diagrams, and websites. As they look at each type of media, students catalog the strengths and weaknesses of these representations before identifying comprehension strategies that can be applied across various media.

Social Studies

1. Invite students to create an underwater map of the Arctic regions, noting which countries claim which natural resources. Students also write an argumentative text in which they explain their definition of "Ice Wars" and predict which country or countries will be successful in claiming the Arctic region/resources. *Recommended resource:* http://www.culturechange.org/cms/content/view/760/1/.

2. Guide students to create a Webquest to explore aspects of climate change in a country or region of their choice. Students participate in research, teamwork, and develop critical thinking, as they complete the Webquest. *Recommended resource:* Global Warming Webquest http://www.climate.gov/teaching/resources/global-warming-webquest

3. Invite students to work in small groups to create PowerPoint Presentations in which they examine the aspects of greenhouse gases and their consequence in various parts of the world. *Recommended resource:* http://news.nationalgeographic.com/news/2012/08/120828-arctic-sea-ice-global-warming-record-environment-science/.

4. Encourage students to read about global warming and microbes that formed millions of years ago and their involvement in global warming. After reading the articles, students hold a classroom Press Conferences in which they share information on a particular topic and address questions from peers. *Recommended resources:* http://news.nationalgeographic.com/news/2012/08/120831-antarctica-methane-global-warming-science-environment/; http://www.noaanews.noaa.gov/stories2009/20090820_alaskaco2.html

English Language Arts

1. Provide journal prompts on climate change, which students will use to write entries in their dialogue journals. Prompts could include: What is climate change? Why is climate change harmful to humans, plants, and animals? How is the greenhouse effect harmful to the earth? *Recommended resource:* http://epa.gov/climatechange/kids/index.html.

2. Organize a Jigsaw-based activity on climate change. Students meet in small groups to read about and discuss one aspect of climate change. Each student will become an "expert" on one topic and then move into a new small group and share his expertise with other students who each have become "experts" on other aspects of climate change. *Recommended resource:* http://epa.gov/climatechange/kids/index.html

3. Engage students in Reader's Theater. Working in small groups, students organize and participate in Reader's Theater, presenting how climate change affects people and the environment. *Recommended resource:* http://epa.gov/climatechange/kids/index.html.

4. Encourage students to create an illustrated timeline, demonstrating the implications of melting ice in the North Pole or other effects of climate change. *Recommended resources:* http://www.independent.co.uk/environment/climate-change/warning-over-melting-ice-

at-north-pole-6268215.html; http://www.usatoday.com/USCP/PNI/Front%20Page/2012-
08-28-BCUSSCIArctic-Sea-Ice1st-LdWritethru_ST_U.htm.

The Arts (Music, Art, Drama)

1. Invite students to create Transmediations (McLaughlin, 2010a) using *climate change* as the focus. Students will self-select their resources.

2. Encourage students to use the project In My Mind's Eye (McLaughlin, 2010a) to create a digital collage of the influence humans have on the global climate. *Recommended resource:* http://www.globalchange.gov.

3. Engage students in Rapping for Review (McLaughlin, 2010a). Students work in small groups to create raps representing their thoughts about methane, carbon, and carbon dioxide in the Arctic regions. *Recommended resource:* http://www.noaanews.noaa .gov/stories2009/20090820_alaskaco2.html.

4. Invite students to write and illustrate form poems (e.g., acrostics, definition poems, cinquains, diamantes) to represent their thoughts about climate change. *Recommended resource:* http://epa.gov/climatechange/kids/index.html.

LESSON PLANS

Examples of two sample rich instructional English Language Arts lessons are included in this section. Both address climate change. Examples of completed strategy applications are included in each lesson. Following the lessons, examples of several unit-related teaching ideas are shared. These include: Discussion Web, K-W-L-S, and PReP, as well as two student writing samples.

Lesson Plan 1

Text: *Learn the Basics: The Earth's Climate Is Changing, and People's Activities are the Main Cause* (http://epa.gov/climatechange/kids/basics/index.html)

Goals and Related CCSS:
Students will:

- Use an Anticipation/Reaction Guide (RI.6.1, 7.1, 8.1)
- Discuss (SL.6.1, 7.1, 8.1).
- Use "I Wonder…" Statements (RI.6.1, 7.1, 8.1; SL.6.1, 7.1, 8.1).
- Create Definition Poems (L.6.1, 7.1, 8.1; W.6.1, 7.1, 8.1).

Engage Students' Thinking:
I began the lesson by discussing climate change. Next, I explained and modeled the Anticipation/Reaction Guide (see Figure A.1). I read the first statement, "Climate change and global warming are the same thing." I said that I disagreed with that statement and asked the

FIGURE A.1 ● Completed Anticipation/Reaction Guide on Climate Change

Agree	Disagree	Statement
	✓	1. Climate change and global warming are the same thing.
✗	✓	2. Humans are the main cause of climate change.
✓		3. Conservation is the best immediate action to reduce greenhouse gases.
✓		4. Humans can lessen the negative effects of climate change.

students if they agreed or disagreed. Then I explained that they would be responding with "agree" or "disagree" to the remaining questions. When all the statements were reviewed, we discussed student responses.

Guide Students' Thinking:

I began by introducing the information article "Learn the Basics: The Earth's Climate Is Changing, and People's Activities Are the Main Cause." Next, we made connections from the text to our completed Anticipation/Reaction Guide. Then I explained to the students that they would be reading the informational article silently and completing "I Wonder…Statements" as they read. I explained that they would have 20 minutes to complete the reading and the "I Wonder…Statements" and then we would have a class discussion based on their wonders and other questions. Samples of students' wonders included:

- Page 1: **I wonder…** why people are concerned about the greenhouse effect, **because…** the greenhouse effect is used to keep the Earth warm.

- Page 5: **I wonder…** why scientists haven't been alarmed about climate changes in the past hundreds of years, **because…** the climate has changed many times before.

Examples of questions related to the text that were raised during discussions included the following: Memory Level: What is climate change? Convergent Level: How do climate change and global warming differ? Divergent Level: If we do nothing to stop climate change, what do you think life will be like 100 years from now? Evaluative Level: Should we, as a society, conserve energy? Defend your response. When our discussion concluded we revisited our Anticipation/Reaction Guide, reviewed our original responses, and marked an "X" to indicate whether our thinking changed after reading the text.

Extend Students' Thinking:

Students extended their thinking by working with partners to create Definition Poems based on climate change topics. After choosing a topic and brainstorming related facts, partners composed their poems. Then partners input their poems in our Electronic Book of Climate Change Poems PowerPoint file and illustrated them. Finally, students used our LCD projector to share and discuss their illustrated poems with the class.

Assessment:
I will:

- review student responses on the Anticipation/Reaction Guides.
- observe students' discussion to monitor quality of responses and participation.
- review and comment on students "I Wonder...Statements."
- view, listen to, and comment on students' electronic Definition Poems and illustrations.

Lesson Plan 2

Text: *Antarctic Methane Could Escape, Worsen Warming* (http://news
             .nationalgeographic.com/news/2012/08/120831-antarctica-methane-global-
             warming-science-environment/)

Goals and Related Standards:
Students will do the following:

- Use a Semantic Question Map (McLaughlin, 2010b) (L.6, 7, 8.4). Discuss (SL.6, 7, 8.1).
- Engage in the strategy Say Something (Short, Harste, & Burke, 1996) (RI.6, 7, 8.1; SL.6, 7, 8.1).
- Create acrostic poems (L.6, 7, 8.4; SL.6, 7, 8.1; W.6, 7, 8.2,4).

Engage Students' Thinking:
Begin the lesson by discussing methane. Next, explain and model use of the Semantic Question Map (see Figure A.2). The focus word for the map is *methane*. Thinking aloud, ask yourself "What is it?" Tell students that you also have other questions about methane, and ask if they can think of additional questions, too. Explain the definition of *methane* and ask students for additional responses.

Ask students to help you respond to the remaining questions. Discuss the questions on the Semantic Question Map, and have students record responses to each question.

Guide Students' Thinking:
Introduce the informational text for this lesson: *Antarctic Methane Could Escape, Worsen Warming* (see URL at beginning of lesson). Help students make connections from the text to their completed Semantic Question Maps.

Explain to students that they will read the article in pairs and participate in Say Something. While students read, invite them to discuss the text with their partners. Students have 20 minutes to complete the reading and engage in Say Something.

FIGURE A.2 ● Completed Semantic Question Map about Methane

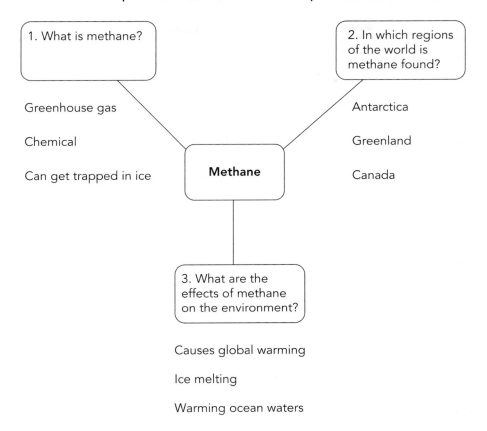

These are examples of ideas students shared during Say Something.

Stopping Point 1
- **Student 1:** I didn't know that methane could be trapped in the ice for millions of years.
- **Student 2:** I knew that methane was a gas, but I didn't know that microorganisms could be trapped in the ice.

Stopping Point 2
- **Student 1:** By sampling pieces of ice from the Antarctic, scientists can estimate if and how much methane is in a particular region.
- **Student 2:** Sampling ice in a lab setting from Antarctica can help determine the amount of methane and microorganisms in the water.

Stopping Point 3

- **Student 1:** I didn't know that millions of years ago, Antarctica was much warmer and was covered with trees.
- **Student 2:** I didn't know that sediment in the mud is producing microbes under the ice today.

Stopping Point 4

- **Student 1:** Microorganisms keep producing methane under the ice, but the methane cannot escape.
- **Student 2:** Because of glacier melting, methane is being released into the atmosphere.

Next, initiate a whole-class discussion, featuring students' Say Something statements as well as other questions. Examples of questions related to the article that might be raised during discussion include the following:

- **Memory level:** What is the definition of *methane?*
- **Convergent level:** How does methane affect the environment?
- **Divergent level:** What do you suppose will happen if the Earth keeps warming at this increased pace?
- **Evaluation level:** Why should scientists study methane? Defend your responses.

Extend Students' Thinking:

To extend students' thinking, have them work with partners to create acrostic poems based on the information from the informational text, as well as other sources. Have students decide their own focus words and then write Acrostic Poems. Finally, ask each pair to read their poem to the class and discuss it with their classmates.

Assessment:

I will:

- Review students' completed Semantic Question Maps.
- Observe students' discussion to monitor quality of responses and participation.
- Review and comment on students' Say Something exchanges.
- Listen to and comment on students' acrostic poems.

EXAMPLES OF UNIT-RELATED STRATEGY APPLICATIONS AND STUDENT WRITING

As noted earlier, this section provides completed examples of several unit-related strategy applications—including a Discussion Web (Alvermann, 1991) (Figure A.3), K-W-L-S (Sippola, 1995) (Figure A.4), and PReP chart (Langer, 1981) (Figure A.5)—as well as two samples of student writing (Figures A.6 and A.7).

FIGURE A.3 ● Completed Discussion Web on Causes of Climate Change

Reasons

Yes

- Scientists have strong evidence that human activity contributes to climate change.
- Global warming is apparent because of burning fossil fuels and deforestation.
- Overabundant amounts of greenhouses gases are released into the atmosphere.
- Large amounts of sea ice are melting.
- Earth is experiencing more hurricanes, heat waves, and droughts.

Discussion Topic/Question
Are humans the major contributors to climate change?

Conclusion
Human activity is the major cause of climate change.

No

- Some scientists and meteorologists disagree with evidence and believe climate change findings are unreliable.
- Earth's climate has always been changing because of natural factors.
- Carbon dioxide (CO_2) is released by "carbon sinks" in the oceans.
- Ocean currents cause warming and cooling.
- Researchers receive grant money for climate change research.

Reason
We came to this conclusion because there is significant scientific evidence supporting that humans are the main contributors to climate change.

ASSESSMENT AND EVALUATION PLAN

Both formative and summative assessments are used throughout the interdisciplinary unit. Examples of formative assessments include observation, informal analysis of student writing, completed strategy applications, artwork, and discussions. Examples of summative assessment include long-term student projects and presentations, formal student writing and research projects, and examinations.

FIGURE A.4 ● Completed K-W-L-S Chart about Climate Change

K (what I know or think I know)	W (what I want to know)	L (what I learned)	S (what I still want to learn)
• Climate is the long weather pattern in a particular area. • Climate change happens slowly over a long period of time. • Human activities are causing changes in the climate. • Global warming is the main reason for climate change. • Ice caps are melting and causing severe weather.	• How does burning fossil fuels create climate change? • Could there be other reasons for climate change? • What are some ways that climate changes affect humans and the environment? • How do scientists know if there are greenhouse gases in the atmosphere?	• Too much carbon dioxide in the atmosphere from burning fossil fuels is bad and making the earth warmer. • Sea ice reflects sunlight and helps keep the earth cool. • People and animals are affected by climate changes such as diseases and animal extinction.	• Can we reverse the effects of climate change? • How many years until there is no more ice in the Arctic? • Will polar bears survive the next hundred years if we do not make changes in global warming?

Text: *A student's guide to global climate change* (http://epa.gov/climatechange/kids/index.html)

FIGURE A.5 ● Completed PReP Chart about Climate Change

Cue idea: Climate Change

Brainstormed Responses	Reasons
1. Global warming 2. Melting glaciers 3. Rising sea levels 4. Animal extinction	1. Earth is warming because of the excess burning of fossil fuels. 2. Global warming has measureable effects. 3. The melting of sea ice has measureable effects. 4. Species of animals will die off if they cannot adapt to new climates and environments.

Text: *A student's guide to global climate change* (http://epa.gov/climatechange/kids/index.html)

FIGURE A.6 ● Unit-Based Student Writing: Sample 1

I can remember growing up and having birthday swimming parties on my actual birthday, May 29. My family lives in a mountainous area and we have always enjoyed the beautiful seasonal weather changes. Every May 29, when I was a child, I would invite all of my friends and family for a big birthday celebration that involved swimming and relaxing. At that time, May was always hot and sunny like a Florida day. During my parties the kids would all go swimming in the warm swimming pool, and the adults would be sipping ice-cold lemonade under the tall oak tree. As I got older and changed, so did the climate in May. I was not sure why this was happening, but I knew it had to do with global warming. The news stations reported that global warming would cause climate changes that would affect the environment. Because of global warming the climate was changing, ice caps were melting, and the world could be in for severe heat waves and droughts.

Although May was hot when I was younger, the news anchor said that the climate was changing due to global warming and seasons will be affected. He said that the reason for global warming was that people are burning fossil fuels and adding greenhouse gases into the atmosphere. Furthermore, climates were usually consistent and people and animals adapted to their climates. Scientists do not know for sure if humans are the main cause of the earth's temperature rising, but it is their theory. As a result, climate patterns are changing.

The climate is not the only thing that is changing due to global warming. Ice caps are also melting leaving animals learning how to adapt or die. The ice melting is a serious issue for plants and animal life. Because there is a variety of species needing a particular climate, changing climates could be devastating. The issue of ice melting in the Arctic is a serious problem and may lead to polar bears only being seen at the zoo.

In addition to the ice caps melting because of global warming, there could be stronger storms, heat waves, and droughts. It makes me realize how vital the topic of global warming is by watching the news. Stronger hurricanes are killing thousands of people and seem to be increasing each year. Also, the people who live on the coasts will be affected by global warming when the sea levels keep rising due to the melting ice.

Even though this all sounds bleak because the climate is changing, the arctic ice is melting, and severe weather patterns are ahead, we need to realize that global warming is being brought on by human activities. We are using fuels for transportation and energy and cutting down forests at staggering rates. Maybe we could lessen global warming by burning less fossil fuel, learning to recycle, and planting more trees. Although these changes will not make the month of May any warmer for my birthday, it will help reduce greenhouse gas emissions and lessen global warming.

FIGURE A.7 ● Unit-Based Student Writing: Sample 2

When thinking about climate change, do we need to be scientists to understand the facts, or can we be people who are just informed? Information is all that anyone needs to realize that our earth is experiencing climate change due to human activities. Does this really matter? And, why should we care? If we are concerned about the environment we live in, then we need to think about the effects of climate change. As a society, we need to care about climate change because it is having negative effects on the environment such as melting sea ice, changing farming patterns, and creating severe tropical storms.

Should we be concerned that increasing sea temperatures are melting the ice covering the Arctic Ocean? We should be worried because the sea ice is what keeps the earth cool by reflecting sunlight back into the atmosphere. While some energy is needed to keep the earth warm, too much sun energy is heating the earth up as astonishing rates. The culprit of global warming is greenhouse gases from the burning of fossil fuels such as coal, oil, and gas. Greenhouse gases are trapping excess heat into the atmosphere, causing the earth to get warmer and melt sea ice.

As a result of the melting sea ice, the oceans are getting warmer and more severe tropical storms are developing. Using a climate model, researchers have been studying the increased strength of hurricanes and the rising water temperatures. They have found that in the past 30 years, ocean temperatures are getting warmer and hurricanes are increasing in strength. This could cause devastation for all people, but especially those who live in coastal areas. Communities need to work together to protect the coastal areas, such as salt marshes and wetlands. These coastal areas help to slow down the water during a hurricane and will reduce the severity of the impact.

Climate change is not only important to people living by the coastline, it can also impact people living in other regions. In the mid-west, there are a lot of crops growing and livestock being raised. If temperatures start to rise too rapidly, it could cause devastation for crops and livestock. The growing season could become longer and some crops may not adapt. Corn and wheat are examples of crops that cannot survive overly hot temperatures. Besides higher temperatures, increased rainfall and droughts can ruin crops and kill animals.

As we have seen, climate change is a major factor in the world we live in. Scientists have been saying for years that we need to cut down on greenhouse gases. And, researchers are providing evidence that humans are the main causes of climate change. Because large ice sheets are melting, farmers are losing crops due to increased rainfall. Droughts and tropical storms are becoming more powerful. Society needs to be concerned about our changing climate.

CULMINATING ACTIVITY

Students will create and hand deliver invitations to their families to our one-hour class event entitled "Celebration to Deter Climate Change: We Can Make a Difference." Students will wear name tags and welcome family members as they arrive. Unit-related refreshments will be provided by parent volunteers, such as Glacier Water, Heat Wave Coffee and Tea, Polar Ice Cream Bars, Climate Cookies, and Climate Change Popcorn.

The event will showcase students' participation in projects and activities across the theme, including Electronic Alphabet Books (McLaughlin, 2010a), PowerPoint presentations, First-Person Experiences (McLaughlin, 2010a), Press Conferences (McLaughlin, 2010a), Reader's Theater performances, and readings of self-authored form poems.

As parents and other visitors leave the celebration, they will be invited to provide written comments about a favorite memory of the event on our We Are Parent Proud Mural or the class computers. Parents will also receive copies of a student-authored poetry collection as thank-you gifts.

RESOURCES

Books for Students

Benoit, P. (2011). *Climate change.* True books: Ecosystems. New York, NY: Children's Press.

Berger Kaye, M. A. C. (2009). *A kids' guide to climate change & global warming: How to take action!* Minneapolis, MN: Free Spirit.

Cherry, L., & Braasch, G. (2010). *How we know what we know about our changing climate: Scientists and kids explore global warming.* Nevada City, CA: Dawn.

David, L., & Gordan, C. (2007). *The down-to-earth guide to global warming.* New York, NY: Orchard Books.

DK Publishing, & Woodward, J. (2008). *Climate change.* DK Eyewitness books. New York, NY: DK Children.

Rockwell, A. (2006). *Why are the ice caps melting? The dangers of global warming.* New York, NY: Collins.

Simon, S. (2010). *Global warming.* New York, NY: Collins.

Books for Teachers

Archer, D., & Rahmstorf, S. (2010). *The climate crisis: An introductory guide to climate change.* New York, NY: Cambridge University Press.

Burroughs, W. J. (2007). *Climate change: A multidisciplinary approach* (2nd ed.). New York, NY: Cambridge University Press.

Mathez, E. A. (2009). *Climate change: The science of global warming and our energy future.* New York, NY: Columbia University Press.

Pilkey, O. H., Pilkey, K. C., & Fraser, M. E. (2011). *Global climate change: A primer.* Durham, NC: Duke University Press.

Robinson, D. G., & Robinson, G. D., III. (2012). *Global warming: Alarmists, skeptics and deniers: A geoscientist looks at the science climate.* Abbeville, SC: Moonshine Cove.

Schmidt, G., & Wolfe, J. (2009). *Climate change: Picturing the science.* New York, NY: W.W. Norton.

Magazines

Junior Scholastic (grades 6–8). Available online at http://classroommagazines.scholastic.com/products/junior-scholastic.

KIDS DISCOVER (ages 7–12). Available online at www.kidsdiscover.com/.

National Geographic Extreme Explorer (grades 6–8). Available online at www.ngsp.com/tabid/672/default.aspx.

Odyssey Magazine for Kids (ages 9–14). Available online at www.cricketmag.com/ODY-ODYSSEY-Magazine-for-Kids-ages-9-14.

Owl (ages 9–13). Available online at http://owlkids.com/owl/index.html.

Ranger Rick (ages 7–14). Available online at www.nwf.org/Kids/Ranger-Rick.aspx.

Scholastic Action (grades 6–12). Available online at http://classroommagazines.scholastic.com/products/scholastic-action.

Science World (grades 6–10). Available online at http://classroommagazines.scholastic.com/products/science-world.

Online Articles

Cooper, C. (2011, Nov. 26). Warning over melting ice at North Pole. *Independent.co.uk.* Retrieved from www.independent.co.uk/environment/climate-change/warning-over-melting-ice-at-north-pole-6268215.html.

Dayton, D. (2011, July 15). Culture change—Ice wars: Burn the riches beneath melting Arctic sea. *CultureChange.org.* Retrieved from www.culturechange.org/cms/content/view/760/1/.

Environmental Protection Agency (EPA). (n.d.). A student's guide to global climate change. *EPA. gov.* Retrieved from http://epa.gov/climatechange/kids/index.html.

Environmental Protection Agency (EPA). (n.d.). Glossary. *EPA.gov.* Retrieved from http://epa.gov/climatechange/kids/glossary.html.

Kunzig, B. (2012, Aug. 31). Antarctic methane could escape, worsen warming. *NationalGeographic.com.* Retrieved from http://news.nationalgeographic.com/news/2012/08/120831-antarctica-methane-global-warming-science-environment/#close-modal.

Rice, D. (2012, Aug. 28). North Pole ice melting much faster this summer. *USAToday.com.* Retrieved from www.usatoday.com/USCP/PNI/Front%20Page/2012-08-28-BCUSSCIArctic-Sea-Ice1st-LdWritethru_ST_U.htm.

Sea Grant, Alaska. (n.d.). Glossary: Alaska Seas and Rivers Curriculum. *Seagrant.uaf.edu.* Retrieved from http://seagrant.uaf.edu/marine-ed/curriculum/glossary.html.

Than, K. (2012, Aug. 28). Arctic Sea ice hits record low—extreme weather to come? *NationalGeographic .com.* Retrieved from http://news.nationalgeographic.com/news/2012/08/120828-arctic-sea-ice-global-warming-record-environment-science/.

Websites

Brain POP (http://chrome.brainpop.com/science/weather/climatetypes/preview.weml)

Eschool Today (www.eschooltoday.com/climate-change/Introduction-to-climate-change-for-children .html)

Kids World (www.kidzworld.com/article/4858-understanding-global-warming)

National Geographic (http://environment.nationalgeographic.com/environment/global-warming)

National Geographic Kids (http://kidsblogs.nationalgeographic.com/greenscene/2010/07/impact-of-global-warming.html)

Science News for Kids (www.sciencenewsforkids.org/2004/11/a-change-in-climate-2/)

U.S. Global Change Research Program (www.global.change.gov)

Weather Wiz Kids (www.weatherwizkids.com/weather-climate.htm)

References

Alvermann, D. (1991). The discussion web: A graphic aid for learning across the curriculum. *The Reading Teacher, 45,* 92–99.

Committee on a Conceptual Framework for New K–12 Science Education Standards, Board on Science Education, Division of Behavioral and Social Sciences and Education, National Research Council. (2012). *A framework for K–12 science education*: *Practices, crosscutting concepts, and core ideas.* Washington, DC: National Academies Press. Retrieved from www.nap.edu/openbook.php?record_id=13165.

Langer, J. (1981). From theory to practice: A prereading plan. *Journal of Reading, 25,* 152–156.

Leu, D. J., & Leu, D. D. (1999). *Teaching with the Internet: Lessons from the classroom* (2nd ed.) Norwood MA: Christopher-Gordon Publishers.

McLaughlin, M. (2010a). *Content area reading: Teaching and learning in an age of multiple literacies.* Boston, MA: Allyn & Bacon.

McLaughlin, M. (2010b). *Guided Comprehension in the primary grades.* Newark, DE: International Reading Association.

National Governors Association Center for Best Practices & Council of Chief State School Officers (NGA & CCSSO). (2010). *Common Core State Standards: English language arts and literacy in history/social studies, science, and technical subjects.* Washington, DC: Authors. Retrieved from www.corestandards.org/assets/CCSSI_ELA%20Standards.pdf.

Next Generation Science Standards (NSTA, 2013). Retrieved from http://www.nextgenscience.org/.

Read-Write-Think. (n.d.). Lesson Plan—Critical Literacy in Action: Multimodal Texts on Global Warming. *Read-Write-Think.org.* Retrieved from www.readwritethink.org/classroom-resources/lesson-plans/critical-literacy-action-multimodal-1139.html.

Short, K., Harste, J., & Burke, C. (1996). *Creating classrooms for authors and inquirers.* Portsmouth, NH: Heinemann.

Sippola, A. E. (1995). K-W-L-S. *The Reading Teacher, 48,* 542–543.

Index

Note: page numbers with *f* indicate figures; those with *t* indicate tables.